"读"有所得

植物与僵尸
Plants and Zombies

主　编　关晓薇　王　倩

副主编　张　博　刘　芳　李　涛

编　委　韩　芳　张力升

大连理工大学出版社
DALIAN UNIVERSITY OF TECHNOLOGY PRESS

图书在版编目（CIP）数据

植物与僵尸：汉英对照 / 关晓薇, 王倩主编. --
大连：大连理工大学出版社, 2012.7
（"读"有所得）
ISBN 978-7-5611-7062-5

Ⅰ.①植… Ⅱ.①关… ②王… Ⅲ.①汉语 – 英语 –
对照读物②散文集 – 中国 – 现代 Ⅳ.①H319.4：I

中国版本图书馆CIP数据核字(2012)第144017号

大连理工大学出版社出版
地址:大连市软件园路80号　　邮政编码：116023
发行：0411-84708842　邮购：0411-84703636　传真：0411-84701466
E-mail:dutp@dutp.cn　　URL: http://www.dutp.cn
辽宁星海彩色印刷有限公司印刷　　　大连理工大学出版社发行

幅面尺寸：168mm×235mm　　　印张：14.75　　　字数：185千字
印数：1~6000
2012年7月第1版　　　　　　　2012年7月第1次印刷

责任编辑：张婵云　　　　　　　　　　　　责任校对：王永华
装帧设计：对岸书影

ISBN 978-7-5611-7062-5　　　　　　　　　定价：24.00元

前　言

　　我们生活在同一个世界，然而每个人的世界又是那么不同。我们改变自己的世界时担当的角色如同大战小僵尸的植物，如果可以坚韧无畏，如果可以耐心平和，那么我们的世界将会从此不同。

　　"让你的世界从此不同"，这正是我们编写此套中英双语读本的目的。本系列共分两册：《天使与魔鬼》和《植物与僵尸》。《植物与僵尸》精选了50篇富含人生哲理的短文，展现了十种植物的优秀品质，这些也正是我们在成长过程中需要拥有的品质。从植物身上，你可以读到从人性里渗透出的各种光芒。让我们的故事给在成长中身处困境和迷惘中的你以最大的鼓舞和最深切的共鸣。

　　在游戏中，僵尸和植物之间，在某天有了难舍难分的关联，他们一个攻一个守，演绎着我们信以为真的故事。我们喜欢初级豌豆的兢兢业业，我们喜欢睡莲的与世无争又踏踏实实，我们更喜欢摇摇摆摆、美滋滋跳着舞的太阳花给生活带来无尽能源……玩罢游戏，现实生活中的我们也像那些可爱的植物，时而坚果般坚忍不拔，时而豌豆般勤勤恳恳，时而太阳花般甘于奉献。只因为我们热爱我们的家园，我们守卫我们的信仰，我们追求美好的生活就要不断努力。

　　我们希望你在赏析美文的同时，提升英文阅读能力；盼望你能思索各色品质的意义，感受生活的魅力与智慧，让你的心灵获得滋养，领悟人生的真谛，在各种历练中慢慢成长。期待你活出不一样的人生！

编者

2012.6

目　录

主观、自信的
向日葵

向日葵篇
I Am Nature's Greatest Miracle

> I will win, for I am unique. I am nature's greatest miracle.
>
> 我会成功，因为我举世无双。我是自然界最伟大的奇迹。

Since the beginning of time never has there been another with my mind, my heart, my eyes, my ears, my hands, my hair, my mouth. None that came before, none that live today, and none that come tomorrow can walk and talk and move and think exactly like me. All men are my brothers yet I am different from each. I am a unique (独一无二的) creature.

Although I am of the animal kingdom, animal rewards alone will not satisfy me. Within me burns a flame, which has been passed from generations uncounted and its heat is a constant irritation (刺激；激励) to my spirit to become better than I am, and I will. I will fan this flame of dissatisfaction and proclaim my uniqueness to the world.

Vain attempts to imitate others no longer will I make. Instead will I place my uniqueness on display in the market place. I will proclaim it, and I will sell it. I will begin now to accent my differences; hide my similarities.

I am a unique creature of nature.

I am rare, and there is value in all rarity; therefore, I am valuable. I am the end product of thousands of years of evolution; therefore, I

2

am better equipped in both mind and body than all the emperors and wise men who preceded me.

But my skills, my mind, my heart, and my body will stagnate (失去活力), rot, and die lest I put them to good use. I have unlimited potential. Only a small portion of my brain do I employ; only a paltry amount of my muscles do I flex. A hundredfold (百倍) or more can I increase my accomplishments of yesterday and this I will do, beginning today.

Nevermore will I be satisfied with yesterday's accomplishments nor will I indulge, anymore, in self-praise for deeds which in reality are too small to even acknowledge (承认). I can accomplish far more than I have, and I will, for why should the miracle which produced me end with my birth? Why can I not extend that miracle to my deeds of today?

I am not on this earth by chance. I am here for a purpose and that purpose is to grow into a mountain, not to shrink to a grain of sand. Henceforth will I apply all my efforts to become the highest mountain of all and I will strain my potential until it cries for mercy.

I have been given eyes to see and a mind to think and now I know a great secret of life for I perceive, at last, that all my problems, discouragements, and heartaches are, in truth, great opportunities in disguise (伪装). I will no longer be fooled by the garments they wear for my eyes are open. I will look beyond the cloth and I will not be deceived (欺骗).

No beast, no plant, no wind, no rain, no rock, no lake had the same beginning as I, for I was conceived in love and brought forth with a purpose. In the past I have not considered this fact but it will henceforth shape and guide my life.

And nature knows not defeat. Eventually, she emerges victorious and so will I, and with each victory the next struggle becomes less difficult.

I will win, for I am unique.

I am nature's greatest miracle. (550 words)

译文

我是自然界最伟大的奇迹

自从上帝创造了天地万物，没有一个人和我一样，我的头脑、心灵、眼睛、耳朵、双手、头发、嘴唇都是与众不同的。言谈举止和我一模一样的人以前没有，现在没有，以后也不会有。虽然四海之内皆兄弟，然而人人各异。我是独一无二的造化。

我不可能像动物一样容易满足，我心中燃烧着代代相传的火焰，它激励我不断超越自己，我要使这团火烧得更旺，向世界宣布我的与众不同。

我不再徒劳地模仿别人，而要展示自己的个性。我不但要宣扬它，还要推销它。我要强调自己的与众不同，回避人的共性。

我是独一无二的奇迹。

物以稀为贵。我特立独行，因而身价百倍。我是千万年进化的终端产物，头脑和身体都超过以往的帝王与智者。

但是，我的技艺，我的头脑，我的心灵，我的身体，若不善加利用，都将逐渐迟钝、腐朽，甚至死亡。我的潜力无穷无尽，脑力、体能稍加开发，就能超过以往的任何成就。从今天开始，我就要开发潜力。

我不再因昨日的成绩沾沾自喜，不再为微不足道的成绩自吹自擂。我能做的比已经完成的更好。我的出生并非最后一样奇迹，为什么自己不能再创奇迹呢？

我不是偶然来到这个世上的。我生来应为高山，而非草芥。从今往后，我要竭尽全力成为群峰之巅，将我的潜能发挥到最大限度。

我有双眼，可以观察；我有头脑，可以思考。现在我已洞悉了一个人一生中的伟大奥秘。我发现，一切问题、沮丧、悲伤，都是乔装打扮的机遇之神。我不再被他们的外表所蒙骗，我已睁开双眼，看破了他们的伪装。

飞禽走兽、花草树木、风雨山石、河流湖泊，都没有像我一样的起源，我孕育在爱中，肩负使命而生。过去我忽略了这个事实，但从今往后，它将塑造我的性格，引导我的人生。

自然界不知何谓失败，终以胜利者的姿态出现。我也要如此，因为成功一旦降临，就会再度光顾。

我会成功，因为我举世无双。

我是自然界最伟大的奇迹。

世界创造了一个独一无二的你，再也没有谁是跟你完全一样的了。在这天地之中，你就是你，无可取代！不要让恐惧、自卑像僵尸一样暗中跟随着你，做一棵自立自信的向日葵吧！积极进取，勇于尝试，努力做最好的自己，让生命在磨砺中焕发出熠熠光彩！

之二

向日葵篇
Being Yourself

You made this day a special day just by being yourself.

你让这一天变得很特别，只是因为你做了你自己。

As a youngster, there was nothing I liked better than Sunday afternoons on my grandfather's farm in western Pennsylvania. Surrounded by miles of winding stone walls, the house and barn provided endless hours of fun for a city kid like me.

I can still remember one afternoon when I was eight years old. Since my first visit to the farm, I had wanted more than anything to be allowed to climb the stone walls. My parents would never agree with me. The walls were old. Some stones were missing and others were loose and crumbling (倒塌). Still, my yearning to climb those walls grew so strong that finally, one spring afternoon, I gathered all my courage and entered the living room, where the adults had gathered after the Sunday dinner.

"I, uh…I want to climb the stone walls," I said hesitantly. Everyone looked up. "Can I climb the stone walls?" Suddenly, a chorus (齐声) went up from the women in the room. "Heavens, no!" they cried. "You'll hurt yourself!" I wasn't too disappointed because the response was just as I had expected. But before I could leave the room, I was stopped by my grandfather's loud voice. "Now hold on just one minute," I heard him say. "Let the boy climb the stone walls.

He has to learn to do things for himself."

"Be careful," he said to me with a wink (眼色), "and come and see me when you get back." For the next two and a half hours I climbed those old walls and had the time of my life. Later I met my grandfather to tell him about my adventures. I'd never forget what he said. "Fred," he said, "you made this day a special day just by being yourself. Always remember, there's only one person in this whole world like you, and I like you exactly as you are."

Consider... YOU! In all time before now and in all time to come, there has never been and will never be anyone just like you. You are unique in the entire history and future of the universe. Wow! Stop and think about that. You're better than one in a million, or a billion, or a gazillion...

You are the only one like you in a sea of infinity (无穷无尽)!

You're amazing! You're awesome! And by the way, you're it. As amazing and awesome as you already are, you can be even more so. Beautiful young people are the whimsy (奇想) of nature, but beautiful old people are true works of art. But you don't become "beautiful" just by virtue of the aging process.

Real beauty comes from learning, growing, and loving in the ways of life. That is the Art of Life. You can learn slowly, and sometimes painfully, by just waiting for life to happen to you. Or you can choose to accelerate (加速) your growth and intentionally devour (挥霍) life and all it offers. You are the artist that paints your future with the brush of today.

Paint a Masterpiece.

God gives every bird its food, but he doesn't throw it into its nest. Wherever you want to go, whatever you want to do, it's truly up to you. (523 words)

(Extracted from "http://en.cnxianzai.com/read.php?tid=66163-fpage=2.html")

译文

做你自己

年少时，再也没有什么比星期天下午呆在爷爷在宾夕法尼亚西部的农场更让我喜欢的了。农舍和谷仓四周环绕着延绵数里的石墙，给了我这样一个城里的孩子无尽的欢乐时光。

我仍然记得在我八岁那年的一个下午。自从我第一次来到农场，我最希望的便是得到允许去爬石墙。我的父母不可能答应我。石墙年代久远了，有些地方缺了石头，其他石头也松松垮垮的，都快塌了。尽管如此，我想爬墙的渴望却变得越发强烈。终于，一个春天的下午，我鼓足勇气走进了大人们星期天吃完晚饭后聚会的客厅。

"我，呃……我想爬那石墙，"我吞吞吐吐地说。所有人都抬起了头看着我。"我可以爬石墙吗？"突然，房间里的女人们齐声说："天哪！不行！"她们喊道，"你会受伤的！"我并不怎么失望，因为我早就预料到会有这种反应了。但是我还没走出房间，就被爷爷洪亮的声音叫住了。"静下来，就一分钟，"我听到他说，"让这孩子去爬石墙吧，他必须学会做他自己想做的事。"

"小心点，"他给我使了一个眼色，"回来后到我这里来。"接下来的两个半小时，我爬上了那些古老的墙，度过了我生命中最快乐的时光。之后，我去爷爷那里告诉他我的冒险经历。我永远不会忘记他所说的话。"弗雷德，"他说，"你让这一天变得很特别，只是因为你做了你自己。要记住：在整个世界上，只有一个像你这样的人，而我喜欢的恰恰就是这个你。"

试想一下……你！一个空前绝后的你，不论是以往还是将来都不会有一个跟你一模一样的人。你在历史上和宇宙中都是独一无二的。哇！想想吧，你是万里挑一、亿里挑一、兆里挑一的。

　　在无穷无尽的宇宙中，你是举世无双的。

　　你是了不起的！你是卓越的！没错，就是你。你已经是了不起的，是卓越的，你还可以更卓越、更了不起。美丽的年轻人是大自然的奇想，而美丽的老人却是艺术的杰作。但你不会因为年龄渐长就自然而然地变得"美丽"。

　　真正的美丽源于生命里的学习、成长和热爱。这就是生命的艺术。你可以只听天由命，慢慢地学，有时候或许会很痛苦。又或许你可以选择加速自己的成长，故意地挥霍生活及其提供的一切。你就是手握今日的画笔描绘自己未来的艺术家。

　　画出一幅杰作吧！

　　上帝给了鸟儿食物，但他没有将食物扔到它们的巢里。不管你想要去哪里，不管你想要做什么，真正做决定的还是你自己。

　　就像世界上没有两片相同的叶子一样，世间每一个人都是绝无仅有、独一无二的。唯其如此，每个人才都有其存在的价值，都有其不可替代的位置。有时，外界的"压力山大"会像一具僵尸立在你的面前，你是否能够像主观、自强的向日葵那样坚定地做你自己呢？相信自己，你的个性你做主！

之三

向日葵篇
To Love Yourself Is the Beginning

If you love yourself, you can jump into your life from a springboard of self-confidence.

如果你爱着自己，你就能从自信的跳板上一跃而起，投入你的生活之中。

A well-known speaker started off his seminar(讲座) by holding up a $20 bill. In the room of 200, he asked, "Who would like this $20 bill?"

Hands started going up. He said, "I am going to give this $20 to one of you, but first, let me do this."

He proceeded to crumple (弄皱) the 20 dollar note up. He then asked, "Who still wants it?" Still the hands were up in the air.

"Well," he replied, "what if I do this?" He dropped it on the ground and started to grind it into the floor with his shoe. He picked it up, now crumpled and dirty.

"Now, who still wants it?"

Still the hands went into the air.

"My friends, you have all learned a very valuable lesson. No matter what I did to the money, you still wanted it because it did not decrease in value. It was still worth $20."

"Many times in our lives, we are dropped, crumpled, and ground into the dirt by the decisions we make and the circumstances that come our way. We feel as though we are worthless; but no matter what happened or what will happen, you will never lose your value."

"Dirty or clean, crumpled or finely creased, you are still priceless to those who love you. The worth of our lives comes, not in what we do or who we know, but by WHO WE ARE."

Therefore, love yourself. Love the things that make you: your values and talents and memories; your clothes, your nose, your woes (悲哀). If you love yourself, you can jump into your life from a springboard (跳板) of self-confidence. If you love yourself, you can say what you want to say, go where you want to go.

The world can be a tough place, and some of the billions of people out there will try to knock you down. Don't join them. Whenever you are feeling low, be your own best friend. Accept that, up to now, you have lived your life the best way you know how. Do things that make you proud, then take pride in what you do and in who you are.

"My great mistake, the fault for which I can't forgive myself," Oscar Wilde wrote, "is that one day I ceased my obstinate (执着的) pursuit of my own individuality (个性)." Keep pursuing your individuality. Keep being yourself. Becoming yourself. It can be comforting to dress and act like everyone else but it is grander to be different, to be unique, to be you.

I'm the only me in the whole wide world.

There is always one true inner voice. Trust it. — Gloria Steinem

"Let me listen to me and not to them," wrote Gertrude Stein. It makes sense to consider the advice and opinions of other people, but don't let their noise drown out (淹没) your inner voice. And don't let the way you sometimes talk or behave in front of others make you lose sight of who you are when you are alone, when you are most you. (504 words)

(Extracted from "http://www.hxen.com/englisharticle/Chicken-Soup/2008-06-07/39901.html")

译文

爱自己是漫步
人生的起点

一位有名的演讲家手里拿着一张20美元的纸币，开始了他的讲座。在200人的屋子里，他问道："谁想要这张20美元纸币？"

开始有人举手。他说："我会把这20美元纸币给你们中的一位，但是，我先要这么做。"

他开始把这张纸币揉皱，然后他问道："还有人想要它吗？"仍然有很多手举在空中。

"好，"他说道，"如果我这样做会怎么样呢？"他把纸币扔到地上，开始用皮鞋使劲地踩。

然后他拣起又脏又皱的纸币，"现在，还有人要它吗？"

空中仍举着很多手。

"朋友们，刚刚你们已经得出一条非常宝贵的经验。不管我怎么糟蹋这张纸币，你们仍然想要它，因为它的价值没有降低。它仍然是20美元。"

"在生活中，很多次我们被自己制定的决策和周边的环境所抛弃、踩踏，甚至碾入尘土。我们感到自己一无是处。但是不管发生了什么，或者将要发生什么，你们永远都不会失去自己的价值。"

"无论你肮脏或者干净，皱巴巴的或者被折磨，对周围爱你的人来说你仍然是无价之宝。我们生活的价值不在于我们做了什么，或者我们认识谁，而在于我们是谁。"

因此，爱你自己以及组成你的一切：你的价值观、才华和回忆；你的衣着、长相和苦恼。如果你爱着自己，你就能从自信的跳板上一跃而起，投入你的生活之中。如果你爱着自己，你就可以说出你想说的话，去你想去的地方。

世界是残酷的，人群中总有一些人想把你打倒。不要与其同流合污。每当你感到失落的时候，你要做自己最亲密的朋友。要承认到目前为止，你是在以你所知的最佳方式生活。做值得让你引以为傲的事情，以你所做的事情为傲，以你自己为傲。

"我最大的错误，我无法原谅自己的那个错误"，奥斯卡·王尔德写道，"就是有一天我放弃了对自我的执着追求。"坚持追求自我个性，坚持做自己，成为你自己。像别人那样打扮和行动也许让人放松，但是更重要的是个性独特，做真正的自己。

在这个广大的世界上，我是唯一的。

总有一个内心真实的声音，相信它。——格洛丽亚·斯泰纳姆

格特鲁德·斯坦曾写过，"让我听自己的而不是听别人的。"考虑他人的建议和想法确实很有道理，但不要让他人的言辞淹没了你内心的声音。并且不要因在他人面前说话行动的方式而丢失真实的自我，在你独处时那个最是你的自我。

要想成功，就不要为自己的缺憾而担忧，不要亦步亦趋地效仿别人，掩饰自己，舍弃自己。只要正视自己，充分发挥自己的才能，就会取得成功。不要让自惭形秽的僵尸把你永远禁锢在阴影里，像自信的向日葵一样沐浴在阳光中吧！相信自己，命运就掌握在自己手中！

之四

向日葵篇
A Place to Stand

Sixteen people dead on the job, and the seventeenth, in precisely the same situation, figured out a way to live.

十六个人呆板地做着工作，而第十七个，几乎处于同样的情况之中，却找到了另外一种生活方式。

If you have ever gone through a toll booth (收费亭), you know that your relationship to the person in the booth is not the most intimate (亲密的) you'll ever have. It is one of life's frequent non-encounters: you hand over some money; you might get change; you drive off. I have been through every one of the 17 toll booths on the Oakland–San Francisco Bay Bridge on thousands of occasions, and never had an exchange worth remembering with anybody.

Late one morning in 1984, headed for lunch in San Francisco, I drove toward one of the booths. I heard loud music. It sounded like a party, or a Michael Jackson concert. I looked around. No other cars with their windows open. No sound trucks. I looked at the toll booth. Inside it, the man was dancing.

"What are you doing?" I asked.

"I'm having a party." he said.

"What about the rest of these people?" I looked over at other booths, nothing moving there.

"They're not invited."

I had a dozen other questions for him, but somebody in a big hurry to get somewhere started punching his horn behind me and I drove off. But I made a note to myself: Find this guy again. There's something in his eye that says there's magic in his toll booth.

Months later I did find him again, still with the loud music, still having a party.

Again I asked, "What are you doing?"

He said, "I remember you from the last time. I'm still dancing. I'm having the same party."

I said, "Look. What about the rest of the people?"

He said, "Stop. What do those look like to you?" He pointed down the row of toll booths.

"They look like toll booths."

"Nooooo imagination!"

I said, "Okay, I give up. What do they look like to you?"

He said, "Vertical (直立的) coffins (棺材)."

"What are you talking about?"

"I can prove it. At 8:30 every morning, live people get in. Then they die for eight hours. At 4:30, like Lazarus from the dead, they reemerge and go home. For eight hours, brain is on hold, dead on the job, going through the motions."

I was amazed. This guy had developed a philosophy (哲学), a mythology (神话) about his job. I could not help asking the next question, "Why is it different for you? You're having a good time."

He looked at me. "I knew you were going to ask that," he said. "I'm going to be a dancer someday." He pointed to the administration (行政) building. "My bosses are in there, and they're paying for my training."

Sixteen people dead on the job, and the seventeenth, in precisely the same situation, figured out a way to live. That man was having a party where you and I would probably not last three days. The boredom! He and I did have lunch later, and he said, "I don't understand why anybody would think my job is boring. I have a corner office, glass on all sides. I can see the Golden Gate, San Francisco, the Berkeley hills; half the Western world vacations are here and I just stroll in every day and practice dancing." (524 words)

(Extracted from "http://www.ebigear.com/news-124-29173.html")

译文

一个人的空间

如果你曾经路过一个收费亭，你就会知道你与亭子里的这个人关系不是最亲密的，这是生命中常常出现的非偶遇者。你递给他一些钱，或许他还要找你些零钱，然后你开车走了。我曾经经过17家收费亭，并在奥克兰-旧金山海湾大桥千百次路过，却没有一次找钱值得我记起某个人。

1984年的一个上午，很晚了，我驱车去旧金山吃午饭，开到一个收费亭旁边，我听到了很响的音乐声。听起来好像在开舞会，或是迈克尔杰克逊的音乐会。我朝四周看了看。别的汽车没有打开窗户的，也没有宣传车。我朝收费亭里望去，有个人在里边跳舞。

"你在干吗？"我问。

"我在开舞会呢。"他说。

"那其他人呢？"我看了看其他的亭子，没什么动静。

"我没邀请他们。"

我还有十几个问题要问他，但我后面的人急着要走，开始按喇叭，我只好开走了。但我在心里告诉自己：还要再找这个人。他眼里有某种东西，告诉我在他的收费亭里有一种魔力。

几个月后我又见到了他，音乐仍然很响，舞会还在进行。

我再次问他："你在做什么呢？"

他说："我记得你上次问过了。我还在跳舞，还在举办同样的舞会。"

我说："瞧，其他人呢？"

"打住。"他说，"你看那些东西像什么呢？"他指着那排收费亭。

"看来就像收费亭啊。"

"真是没有想象力！"

我说："那好，我放弃。你看它们像什么呢？"

他说："直立的棺材。"

"你在说些什么呀？"

"我可以证明。每早八点半，活人走进去，之后的八个小时他们是死的。下午四点半，就像死人中的拉撒路，他们复活回到家中。整整八个小时，头脑思维中断，他们只是呆板地工作，重复着相同的动作。"

我感到非常惊异。这个小伙子发展了一种哲学，创造了一个有关工作的神话。我禁不住又问了一个问题，"为什么你不一样？你过得很快乐。"

他看了看我，"我就知道你会问这个，"他接着说，"总有一天我会成为一个舞蹈家。"他指向行政机关大楼："我的老板都在那里，他们花钱为我培训。"

十六个人呆板地做着工作，而第十七个，几乎处于同样的情况之中，却找到了另外一种生活方式。那个人所举办的舞会，你我恐怕连三天都坚持不了。无聊！他和我后来确实一起吃过午饭，他说："我不明白为什么每个人都认为我的工作很枯燥。我有一个街角办公室，四周都是玻璃。我可以看见金门海峡、旧金山和伯克利山，半个西方世界都在这儿度假，每天我只是漫步到这里，练习跳舞。"

如果自暴自弃的想法像僵尸一样对你说：你的条件比别人差，运气没有别人好，家庭环境不够优越……那么就做向日葵，用自信、勇敢的法宝击败它！"天生我材必有用"。也许你不能成为将军，但你能使自己成为最好的士兵；也许你不能成为伟人，但你完全可以活出一个优秀的自己！

向日葵篇
Get a Thorough Understanding
of Oneself

To get a thorough understanding of oneself is to get
a full control of one's life.

彻悟了自己，你才能把握自己的生命。

In all one's lifetime, it is oneself that one spends the most time being with or dealing with. But it is precisely oneself that one has the least understanding of. When you are going upwards in life you tend to overestimate yourself. When you are going downhill you tend to underestimate yourself. It's likely that you think it is wise for yourself to know your place and stay aloof (远离的) from world wearing a mask of cowardice (懦弱), behind which the flow of sap in your life will be retarded (减慢).

People say they'd like to do this or that, but… Then they offer all the excuses in the world why they can't do whatever "it" is. No matter what the excuses are, the only thing usually limiting them is their own self-perception (自我认知).

If your self-perception is that you can't accomplish something because you're not smart enough, then take the time to learn what you need to know and your self-perception will change.

If your self-perception is that you can't accomplish something because you never finish anything you start, then go finish something and change your self-perception.

If your self-perception is that you're too lazy, too busy, too unworthy, too unfocused, too depressed, too dependent on others, too anything to accomplish great things, then you're right. You are that because you believe that, but you can change that!

To get a thorough understanding of oneself is to gain a correct view of oneself and be a sober realist — aware of both one's strength and shortage. You may look forward hopefully to the future but be sure not to expect too much, for ideals can never be fully realized. You may be courageous to meet challenges but it should be clear to you where to direct your efforts.

To get a thorough understanding of oneself needs self-appreciation (自我欣赏). Whether you liken yourself to a towering tree or a blade of grass, whether you think you are a high mountain or a small stone, you represent a state of nature that has its own reason of existence. If you earnestly admire yourself, you will have a real sense of self-appreciation, which will give you confidence. As soon as you gain full confidence in yourself, you will be enabled to fight and overcome any adversity (灾难).

To get a thorough understanding of oneself also requires doing oneself a favor when it's needed. In time of anger, do yourself a favor by giving vent (发泄) to it in a quiet place so that you won't be hurt by its flames; in time of sadness, do yourself a favor by sharing it with your friends so as to change a gloomy mood into a cheerful one; in time of tiredness, do yourself a favor by getting a good sleep or taking some tonic. Show yourself loving concern about your health and daily life. Unless you know perfectly well when and how to do yourself a favor, you won't be confident and ready enough to resist the attack of illness.

To get a thorough understanding of oneself is to get a full

control of one's life. Then one will find one's life full of color and flavor. (524 words)

彻悟自我

人生在世，和自己相处的时间最多，打交道最多，但是人最不了解的也恰恰是自己。当你一帆风顺时，往往高估自己；不得志时，又往往低估自己。你可能认为安分守己、与世无争是明智之举，而实际上往往被怯懦的面具窒息了自己鲜活的生命。

有人会说，他喜欢这喜欢那，但是……然后便给出他所能找到的各种理由来解释他为什么没能去做这些事。但无论是什么借口，通常唯一能限制他们的只有他们的自我认知。

如果你的自我认知是你因不够聪明而不能完成某件事情，那么就花时间去学习你所需要的知识，这样，你的自我认知就会改变。

如果你的自我认知是你因做事常半途而废而不能完成某件事情，那么就去做完它，改变这种自我认知。

如果你的自我认知是你因太懒惰、太忙、太卑微、太不专心、太消沉、太依赖别人，太这太那而不能做成大事，那么你是对的。

你确实是这样，因为你自己就是这样认为的，但你可以改变这种状态。

彻悟自己，就是正确认识自己。做一个清醒的现实主义者，既知道自己的优势，也知道自己的不足。我们可以憧憬人生，但不要期望过高。因为在现实中，理想的实现总是会打折扣的。你可以勇敢地迎接挑战，但是必须清楚自己努力的方向。

要彻悟自己就要欣赏自己。无论你是一棵参天大树，还是一棵无名小草，无论你想成为一座高山，还是一块石头，你都是一种自然存在，都有自己存在的理由。只要你认真地欣赏自己，你就会真正学会自我欣赏，你才会拥有信心。一旦拥有了信心，你就能战胜任何灾难。

要彻悟自己，就要善待自己。在气愤时善待自己，找个僻静之处宣泄一下，不要因那些无名之火伤身；忧伤时，要善待自己，找个好友倾诉一番，让低迷的情绪高涨起来；劳累时，你要善待自己，睡个好觉或者吃点滋补品，对自己的健康和生活关心备至。唯有清楚地知道如何善待自己，你才会信心百倍，从容不迫地应对疾病的侵袭。

彻悟了自己，你才能把握自己的生命，你的生活才会丰富多彩、有滋有味！

人生道路上一定有许多坎坷、磨难像僵尸一样无法绕过，你是否能像向日葵那样用自信这把锋利的剑把它们斩断呢？面对挫折能够保持一种恬淡平和的心境，是彻悟人生的大度。自信的花朵开放在每个人的心中，就看你是与它擦肩而过，还是紧紧抓住。

坚韧、顽强的高坚果

之一

坚果篇

There Are No Such Setbacks That We Couldn't Overcome!

We will only get to realize our own iron will and strong tolerating ability after getting stricken heavily.

人总是在遭遇一次重创之后，才会幡然醒悟，重新认识自己的坚强和坚忍。

Our tolerating ability is indeed beyond our imagination. But not until the very critical moment will we realize our potential tolerating ability.

There was a woman in the countryside who got married at the age of 18 and had to escape with her two daughters and a son wherever she could at the age of 26 due to the Japanese army's invasion. Many people in the village at that time could not bear the suffering of being a fugitive (逃亡者) and wanted to commit suicide. After she knew about it, she would come to those people and soothed (安慰) them by saying, "Don't do that silly thing. There are no such setbacks (挫折) that we could not overcome. The Japanese armies are bound to be foiled one day!"

Finally she insisted until the day when all the Japanese armies were kicked out of China. Nonetheless, her son died of disease without sufficient medicine and nutrition in those days of hardships. Her husband, after knowing the death of his son, lay in bed for two days without eating and drinking anything. She tore to her husband and said, "We have a tough destiny, but however tough our lives will be, we should also persist. Though our son has passed away, we can have another. There are no such setbacks that we could not overcome."

After giving birth to the second son, her husband died of edema (水肿), which almost blew her away. But eventually, she recovered and cuddled (搂抱) the three young children, saying, "My sweet hearts, don't feel scared. You still have me, your dear mum!"

It took her painstaking efforts to raise her children up and the life of her family was getting better and better. Two daughters were married and so was his son finally. She said to everyone she met, "Look! What I said is absolutely right. There are no such setbacks that we could not overcome! My life is so happy now!" She was aging gradually and could not do the farm work any more. So she stayed at home and did some stitching (缝纫) work.

Nevertheless, the Heaven seemed to show no affection to her who had undergone a rough life. She got her leg broken accidentally when she was nursing her grandson. Due to her old age that posed a great risk to her operation, she did not receive operation and had to lie in bed all day long. Her children all cried heavily, while she merely said, "Why do you cry? I am still living."

Even though she could not rise from bed, she did not complain about anything and anybody. Instead, she sat on the bed and did some stitching work. She had learnt scarves-weaving, broidery (刺绣), crafts-making, etc. All her neighbors spoke highly of her skills and came to learn from her.

She lived until 86. Before she went to Heaven, she said to her children, "You all should live to your best. There are no such setbacks that we could not overcome!"

We will only get to realize our own iron will and strong tolerating ability after getting stricken heavily. Therefore, no matter what you are suffering from now, do not merely complain about the unfairness of our destiny and maintain low–spirited all the time. There are no such setbacks that we could not overcome. Only those who have no confidence and courage to overcome setbacks will be defeated at last! (565 words)

译文

没有过不去的坎儿

人的承受能力，其实远远超出我们的想象。但是不到关键时刻，我们很少能够意识到自己的潜力。

有一位农村妇女，18岁结婚，26岁时日本人侵略中国，在农村进行大扫荡，她不得不经常带着两个女儿一个儿子东躲西藏。村里很多人受不了这种暗无天日的折磨，想到了自尽，她得知后就会去劝他们，"别干傻事儿，没有过不去的坎儿，日本鬼子不会总这么猖狂的。"

她终于熬到了把日本鬼子赶出中国的那一天，可是她的儿子却在那炮火连天的岁月里，由于缺医少药，又极度缺乏营养，因病夭折了。丈夫不吃不喝在床上躺了两天两夜，她流着泪对丈夫说："咱们的命苦啊，不过再苦咱也得过啊，儿子没了，咱再生一个，人生没有过不去的坎儿。"

刚刚生了二儿子，丈夫患水肿离开了人世。在这个打击下，她很长时间都没回过神来，但最后还是挺过来了，她把三个未成年的孩子揽到自己怀里，说："娘还在呢，有娘在，你们就别怕。"

她含辛茹苦地把孩子一个个拉扯大了，生活也慢慢好转起来。两个女儿嫁了人，儿子也结了婚。她逢人便乐呵呵地说："我说吧，没有过不去的坎儿，现在生活多好啊！"她年纪大了，不能再下地干活，就在家缝缝补补。

可是，上苍似乎并不眷顾这位一生坎坷的妇女，照看孙子时她不小心摔断了腿。由于年纪太大做手术很危险，她就一直没有做手术，每天只能躺在床上。儿女们都哭了，她却说："哭什么，我还活着呢。"

即便下不了床，她也没有怨天尤人，而是坐在床上做针线活。她会织围巾，会绣花，会编手工艺品。左邻右舍的人都夸她手艺好，还来跟她学艺。

她活到86岁，临终前，她对儿女们说："都要好好过啊，没有过不去的坎儿！"

人总是在遭遇一次重创之后，才会幡然醒悟，重新认识自己的坚强和坚忍。所以，无论你正在遭受什么磨难，都不要一味抱怨上苍不公平，甚至从此一蹶不振。人生没有过不去的坎儿，只有过不去的人。

人生并不是一帆风顺的，总会遇到一些难过的坎儿，重要的是怎样对待磨难。你需要有坚韧的品格来对待困难，你需要在磨难中锻炼你坚韧的品格。不管在生活中遇到什么困难，你都要做坚忍不拔、百折不挠的坚果，勇敢地向脆弱的僵尸挑战。"人生没有过不去的坎儿，只有过不去的人。"

坚果篇
I Will Persist Until I Succeed

> So long as there is breath in me, that long will I persist.
>
> 只要我一息尚存，就要坚持到底。

The prizes of life are at the end of each journey, not near the beginning; and it is not given to me to know how many steps are necessary in order to reach my goal. Failure I may still encounter at the thousandth step, yet success hides behind the next bend in the road. Never will I know how close it lies unless I turn the corner.

Always will I take another step. If that is of no avail I will take another, and yet another. In truth, one step at a time is not too difficult.

Henceforth, I will consider each day's effort as but one blow of my blade against a mighty oak. The first blow may cause not a tremor (颤动) in the wood, nor the second, nor the third. Each blow, of itself, may be trifling, and seem of no consequence. Yet from childish swipes (猛击) the oak will eventually tumble. So it will be with my efforts of today.

I will remember the ancient law of averages and I will bend it to my good. I will persist with knowledge that each failure to sell will increase my chance for success at the next attempt. Each nay I hear will bring me closer to the sound of yea. Each frown I meet only prepares me for the smile to come. Each misfortune I encounter will carry in it the seed of tomorrow's good luck. I must have the night to appreciate the day. I must fail often to succeed only once.

I will try, and try, and try again. Each obstacle I will consider as a mere detour (绕弯) to my goal and a challenge to my profession. I will persist and develop my skills as the mariner develops his, by learning to ride out the wrath of each storm.

Henceforth, I will learn and apply another secret of those who excel in my work. When each day is ended, not regarding whether it has been a success or a failure, I will attempt to achieve one more sale. When my thoughts beckon (引诱) my tired body homeward I will resist the temptation to depart. I will try again. I will make one more attempt to close with victory, and if that fails I will make another. Never will I allow any day to end with a failure. Thus will I plant the seed of tomorrow's success and gain an insurmountable (不能超越的) advantage over those who cease their labor at a prescribed (指定的) time. When others cease their struggle, the mine will begin, and my harvest will be full.

Nor will I allow yesterday's success to lull me into today's complacency (满足), for this is the great foundation of failure. I will forget the happenings of the day that is gone, whether they were good or bad, and greet the new sun with confidence that this will be the best day of my life.

So long as there is breath in me, that long will I persist. For now I know one of the greatest principles of success: if I persist long enough I will win.

I will persist. I will win. (520 words)

(Extracted from "http://www.hxen.com/englisharticle/yingyumeiwen/2010-07-31/117139.html")

译文

坚持不懈，
直到成功

生命的奖赏远在旅途终点，而非起点附近。我不知道要走多少步才能到达目标。踏上第一千步的时候，仍然可能遭遇失败。但成功就藏在拐角后面，除非拐了弯，我永远不知道还有多远。

再前进一步，如果没有用，就再向前一步。事实上，每次进步一点点并不太难。

从今往后，我会将每天的奋斗看成对参天大树的一次砍击，头几刀可能了无痕迹。每一击看似微不足道，然而，累积起来，巨树终会倒下。这恰如我今天的努力。

我要牢牢记住古老的平衡法则，鼓励自己坚持下去，因为每一次的失败都会增加下一次成功的机会。这一次的拒绝就是下一次的赞同，这一次皱起的眉头就是下一次舒展的笑容。今天的不幸，往往预示着明天的好运。夜幕降临，回想一天的遭遇，我总是心存感激。我深知，只有失败多次，才能成功。

我要尝试，尝试，再尝试。障碍是我成功路上的弯路，我迎接这项挑战。我要像水手一样，乘风破浪。

从今往后，我要借鉴别人成功的秘诀。过去的是非成败，我全不计较，只抱定信念，明天会更好。当我精疲力竭时，我要抵制回家的诱惑，再试一次。我一试再试，争取每一天的成功，避免以失败收场。我要为明天的成功播种，超过那些按部就班的人。在别人停滞不前时，我继续拼搏，终有一天会获得丰收。

我不因昨日的成功而满足，因为这是失败的先兆。我要忘却昨日的一切，不管是好是坏，都让它随风而去。我信心百倍，迎接新的太阳，相信今天是此生最好的一天。

只要我一息尚存，就要坚持到底。如今我已深知成功的秘诀：只要我坚持得足够长久，我就会成功。

坚持不懈，终会成功。

"骐骥一跃，不能十步；驽马十驾，功在不舍。"成功的秘诀不在于一蹴而就，而在于你是否能够持之以恒。前方的路充满荆棘和考验，就像一具具僵尸无法逾越，你是否敢做坚强不屈的坚果勇敢面对、迎难而上？坚持不懈才会有梦想和希望，它会让你的人生丰富而精彩！

坚果篇

Hold Your Dream and Never Give up

Instead of making dozens of excuses why you cannot realize your dreams, just hold your dream and never give up.

与其找借口解释梦想为什么不能实现，不如坚持你的梦想，永不放弃。

The adolescent girl from Tennessee was standing on the stage of a drama summer camp in upstate (北部的) New York. It was a beautiful day. But the girl didn't feel beautiful. She was not the leggy, glamorous (迷人的) Hollywood type. In fact, she described herself as dorky (笨；傻).

Since she was six years old, Reese Witherspoon had wanted to be a country singer. And Dolly Parton was her idol. But this flat-chest wisp of a girl was not Dolly Parton. Nevertheless, all of this summer she had been acting, dancing and singing — giving it her best. "If you're going to make it in this business, it's not going to be on sexy. Better focus on what you're good at." She thought.

Despite three years of lessons, at the end of camp her coaches told her to forget about singing. They suggested she think about another career. If Reese did have talent, it was hiding under her skinny, mousy frame and her Coke-bottle glasses.

Still, she took their words to heart. After all, why shouldn't she believe the professionals?

But back at home in Nashville, her mother — a funny, happy,

upbeat person — wouldn't let her mope (消沉). Her father, a physician, encouraged her to achieve in school. So she worked hard at everything and was accepted at Stanford University.

And at age 19, she got a part in a low-budget movie called Freeway. That led to a substantial (重要的) role in the movie Pleasantville. But her big break came with Legally Blonde.

Well, she decided, "if you can't sing and you aren't glamorous, play to your strengths. If you're going to make it in this business, it's not going to be on sexy — that's not who you are. Better focus on what you're good at. Celebrate yourself." And then came the offer that took her back to her Nashville roots — playing the wife of tormented (饱受折磨的) country star Johnny Cash. A singing role.

All of a sudden the old fears were back. She was so nervous on the set, a reporter wrote, she "kept a sick bucket" nearby and admitted she "would go backstage after a singing scene and shake". But she didn't give up on the movie or herself.

The humor and drive she learned at home overcame the self-doubt learned on that summer stage. She spent 6 months taking singing lessons again. She learned to play the autoharp (竖琴). And the hard work built up her confidence.

Last March, Reese Witherspoon walked up on another stage, the Kodak Theatre in Hollywood, and accepted the Oscar as Best Actress for her heartbreaking, heartwarming singing role as June Carter Cash in Walk the Line.

Finally, as you read these accounts of Reese Witherspoon, consider the obstacles she met. You've got to have a dream. When you lose your dreams, you die. We have so many people walking around who are dead and don't even know it. The lesson of the story is that instead of making dozens of excuses why you cannot realize your dreams, think about this story, just hold your dream and never give up. If you carry on, one day something good will happen. Something wouldn't have happened if not for that previous disappointment. (529 words)

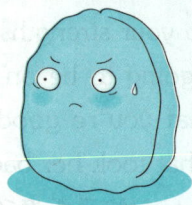

译文

坚持梦想
永不放弃

一名少女由田纳西州来到纽约北部，她站在戏剧夏令营的舞台上，虽然天气是那么好，她的心情却一点也不好。因为她不是那种身材颀长、丰腴美艳的好莱坞式美女，实际上她形容自己是"土里土气，还有点儿傻"。

从六岁开始，里斯·威瑟斯庞就梦想着成为一名乡村歌手，多丽·帕顿是她心中的偶像。但她一点儿都不像多丽·帕顿，她胸部扁平，身材纤细。然而，整个夏天她都在尽全力地表演、跳舞和唱歌。她想："如果想在这一行发展，不要走自己不擅长的性感路线，而要更好地专注于自己的特长。"

她已经上了三年的声乐课程，但夏令营结束时，老师们还是建议她应该忘掉唱歌这件事儿，另谋出路。如果说里斯确实有天分的话，那也被她纤细的身材和厚如可乐瓶底儿的眼镜给遮盖住了。

虽然心有不甘，可她还是听从了建议，毕竟，她有什么理由怀疑专业人士呢？

但回到位于纳什维尔的家里，她的妈妈—— 一个风趣、快乐、乐观的人——可不会让里斯感到丝毫的沮丧。她的爸爸是一名医生，他鼓励女儿在学业上有所成就。于是，她凡事努力，终于被斯坦福大学录取。

19岁那年，她出演了一部低成本电影《极速惊魂》。这为她后来在电影《欢乐谷》中争取到真正重要的角色奠定了基础。而她真正的破冰之作是影片《律政俏佳人》。

她暗下决心："既然自己没有歌唱天分，又不是光彩照人，那就发挥长处。要想在这行做下去，就不要在性感上做文章了——自己不是那种类型的。最好在自己擅长的方面下功夫。为自己喝彩。"这时，她接到片约，邀她出演约翰尼·卡什——一个饱受折磨的乡村歌手——的妻子，这是个需要演员有唱功的角色。她又回到了家乡纳什维尔。

突然，旧时所有的恐惧感又回来了。一名记者报道说，她在台上实在是太紧张了，甚至在一边"准备了呕吐时要用的痰盂"，她自己也承认"每唱完一幕回到后台，自己都在发抖"。但她没放弃那部电影，也没放弃自己。

在温暖的家中获得的幽默感和强大的动力让她战胜了自卑。她用六个月的时间重新开始学习声乐。她还学会了演奏竖琴。不懈的努力让她重拾信心。

去年3月，里斯·威瑟斯庞走上了另一个舞台——好莱坞的柯达剧院。凭借在影片《一往无前》里饰演的琼·卡特·卡什这一歌唱角色，她获得了奥斯卡最佳女演员奖，她在片中饰演的角色令人心碎，但也让人感到温暖。

　　最后，当你读里斯·威瑟斯庞的故事时，想想她遇到的挫折。你一定要有梦想。失去了梦想，人就死了。在我们周围有那么多行尸走肉般的人，他们却不自知。这个故事告诉我们，与其找借口解释梦想为什么不能实现，不如想想这个故事，坚持你的梦想，永不放弃。如果你坚持下去，总有一天会有好事发生。如果没有以前的挫折，就不会有现在的一切。

　　实现梦想的过程中，可能会有无数次失败，面对这些强大的僵尸，你能做坚定、顽强的坚果，勇敢地同它们作战吗？只要你抬头看着你的梦想，坚持梦想，不断探索，不断创新，让梦想激发生命中更多的潜能，梦想总会有实现的一天。在这个绽放梦想的时代，脚踏实地，百折不挠。坚持成就梦想！

坚果篇
Broken Wings, Flying Heart

Tough times never last, but tough people do. Tough people stick it out.

艰难的岁月不会没完没了，坚韧的人却会始终不懈，坚持到底。

He lost his arms in an accident that claimed his father's life—who was the main source of support for the family. Since then, he has had to depend on the arms of his younger brother. For the sake of taking care of him, his younger brother became his shadow, never leaving him alone for years. Except for writing with his toes, he was completely unable to do anything in his life.

One late night, he suffered from diarrhea (腹泻) and had to wake up his younger brother. His younger brother accompanied him into the toilet and then went back the dorm to wait. But being so tired, his younger brother fell asleep, leaving him on the toilet for two hours till the teacher on duty discovered him. As the two brothers grew up together, they had their share of problems and they would often quarrel. Then one day, his younger brother wanted to live separate from him, living his own life, as many normal people do. So he was heart-broken and didn't know what to do.

A similar misfortune befell (降临) a girl, too. One night her mother, who suffered from chronic (慢性的) mental illness disappeared. So her father went out looking for her mother, leaving her alone at home. She tried to prepare meals for her parents, only to overturn the kerosene (煤油) light on the stove, resulting in a fire which took her hands away.

Though her elder sister who was studying in another city, showed her willingness to take care of her, she was determined to be completely independent. At school, she always studied hard. Most of all she learned to be self-reliant. Once she wrote the following in her composition: "I am lucky. Though I lost my arms, I still have legs; I am lucky. Though my wings are broken, my heart can still fly."

One day, the boy and the girl were both invited to appear on a television interview program. The boy told the TV host about his uncertain future at being left on his own, whereas the girl was full of enthusiasm for her life. They both were asked to write something on a piece of paper with their toes. The boy wrote: My younger brother's arms are my arms. While the girl wrote: Broken wings, flying heart.

They had both endured the same ordeal (苦难), but their different attitudes determined the nature of their lives. It is true that life is unpredictable (无法预料的). Disasters can strike at any time. How you handle misfortune when confronted with it is the true test of your character. If you choose only to complain and escape from the ordeal, it will always follow you wherever you go. But if you decide to be strong, the hardship will turn out to be a fortune on which new hopes will arise.

Tough times never last, but tough people do. Tough people stick it out. Whatever you're going through, tell yourself you can handle it. Compared to what others have been through, you're fortunate. Tell this to yourself over and over, and it will help you get through the rough spots with a little more fortitude (坚毅). (522 words)

(Extracted from "http://en.cnxianzai.com/read.php?tid-25725-fpage-11.html")

翅膀断了，
心也要飞翔

在一次事故中，他失去了双手，作为家中顶梁柱的父亲也永远地离去了。从此弟弟的手便成了他的手。为了照顾他，弟弟从小到大总是形影不离地跟在他的身边，他除了学会用脚趾头写字之外，生活上完全不能自理。

有一次，他肠胃不好，半夜起来要上厕所，于是他叫醒了弟弟。弟弟帮着他进了厕所后，就回宿舍去等。由于太劳累，弟弟闭上眼就睡着了。结果他在厕所里等了整整两个小时，才被查夜的老师发现。慢慢长大了的两兄弟也有了烦恼和争执。有一天弟弟终于提出要离开他，因为弟弟和很多正常人一样需要过自己的生活。为此，他很伤心，不知如何是好。

无独有偶，另一个女孩也有着同样的遭遇。长期患有精神病的妈妈在一天晚上无故出走，爸爸去找妈妈了，家中便只留下她一人。她决定做好饭菜等爸爸妈妈回来吃，却不小心将灶台上的煤油灯打翻，结果双手便被大火夺走了。

虽然在外地读书的姐姐愿意照顾她，可倔强的她一定要自己照顾自己。在学校，她不但读书认真，更重要的是她学会了生活自理。她曾在一篇作文里写道："我很幸运，虽然失去了双手，但我还拥有一双脚；我很幸运，虽然翅膀断了，但心也要飞翔。"

有一天，男孩和女孩都被一家电视台邀请到了演播室。面对主持人，男孩表现出了独自面对前途的迷茫，而女孩则对生活充满了热情。主持人要求他们分别在一张白纸上写一句话。他们都用脚趾头夹起了笔，男孩写的是：弟弟的手便是我的手。女孩却写下了：翅膀断了，心也要飞翔。

他们俩都经受了同样的苦难，但不同的人生态度却决定了其生活的本质。是的，人生多变幻，苦难总是在不知不觉中骤然降临。如何应对苦难，是对你的性格的真正考验。面对苦难，如果选择抱怨与逃避，苦难就永远如影随形；但如果选择坚强，苦难便会化作甘泉，滋润美好的希望。

艰难的岁月不会没完没了，坚韧的人却会始终不懈，坚持到底。无论你遭遇了什么，你都要对自己说：一定能挺过去的。和其他人的不幸相比，你已经算幸运了。要一遍遍地用这些话鼓励自己，这个信念将会使你更有决心去渡过难关。

落在瓦砾中的有生命的种子决不会悲观叹气，它相信有了阻力才有磨练，它能用斗志和坚韧来创造自己所能创造出的辉煌。漫漫人生路，不如意者十有八九。做一个坚韧、顽强的坚果，去击败怨天尤人的僵尸吧！只有在拼搏过程中，不断坚持，不断进取，才能让我们的生命更加美丽、绚烂！

坚果篇
I Tell Myself I Can Handle It

> I tell myself I can handle it. Compared to what others have been through, I'm fortunate.
>
> 我跟自己说我一定可以捱过去的。跟别人的遭遇相比，我已经算是幸运的了。

What is the secret ingredient (要素) of tough people that enables them to succeed? Why do they survive the tough times when others are overcome by them? Why do they win when others lose? Why do they soar when others sink?

The answer is very simple. It's all in how they perceive their problems. Yes, every living person has problems. A problem—free life is an illusion — a mirage in the desert.

In 1982 Steven Callahan was crossing the Atlantic alone in his sailboat when it struck something and sank. He was out of the shipping lanes and floating in a life raft, alone. His supplies were few. His chances were small. Yet when three fishermen found him seventy—six days later (the longest anyone has survived a shipwreck on a life raft alone), he was alive — much skinnier than he was when he started, but alive.

His account of how he survived is fascinating. How he ingeniously (巧妙地) managed to catch fish, how he fixed his solar still, which evaporates (蒸发) seawater to make fresh water, is very interesting.

But the thing that caught my eye was how he managed to keep himself going when all hope seemed lost, when there seemed no point in continuing the struggle, when he was suffering greatly, when his life raft was punctured (刺穿) and after more than a week struggling with his weak body to fix it, it was still leaking air and wearing him out to keep pumping it up. He was starved. He was desperately dehydrated (脱水). He was thoroughly exhausted. Giving up would have seemed the only sane option.

When people survive these kinds of circumstances, they do something with their minds that gives them the courage to keep going. Many people in similarly desperate circumstances give in or go mad. Something the survivors do with their thoughts helps them find the guts to carry on in spite of overwhelming (势不可挡的) odds.

"I tell myself I can handle it," wrote Callahan in his narrative. "Compared to what others have been through, I'm fortunate. I tell myself these things over and over, building up fortitude (坚毅，不屈不挠)."

I wrote that down after I read it. It struck me as something important. And I've told myself the same thing when my own goals seemed far off or when my problems seemed too overwhelming. And every time I've said it, I have always come back to my senses.

The truth is, our circumstances are only bad compared to something better. But others have been through much worse. I've read enough history to know you and I are lucky to be where we are, when we are, no matter how bad it seems to us compared to our fantasies. It's a sane thought and worth thinking.

Every mountain has a peak. Every valley has its low point. Life has its ups and downs, its peaks and its valleys. No one is up all the time, nor are they down all the time. Problems do end. They are all resolved in time. You may not be able to control the times, but you can compose your response. You can turn your pain into profanity (亵渎) — or into poetry. The choice is up to you. (529 words)

我可以挺过去

坚忍不拔的人成功的秘诀是什么？他们为什么能挺过艰难的时刻，而其他人却被困难所压倒？为什么他们成功了，而其他人却失败了？为什么他们一飞冲天，而其他人都深陷泥沼？

答案很简单，全看他们是如何看待自己面临的难题。不错，人人有本难念的经。没有难题困扰的人生只能是一个幻想，是沙漠中的海市蜃楼。

1982年史蒂文·卡拉汉独自驾驶着帆船横渡大西洋，途中帆船触礁下沉。他在救生艇里孤独地漂浮着，远离了航道。当时他身上的食物所剩无几，生存机会非常渺茫。但76天后，三个渔民发现了他，他还活着（他是世界上遭遇海难，在救生艇上存活时间最长的人），他当时瘦骨嶙峋，与出航前相比简直判若两人，然而他还活着。

关于他大难不死的故事让人惊叹。其中他是如何巧妙地抓鱼，如何固定太阳蒸馏器来提取淡水的事情都非常有趣。

但我最感兴趣的还是在他感到彻底绝望的时候，当一切抗争似乎都已毫无意义的时候，当灾难苦苦折磨着他的时候，他是如何支撑着活下来的？救生艇穿了洞，他强撑着虚弱的身体，花了一周多的时间去修理，可救生艇仍然漏气，于是他耗尽了所有的力气去吹气。饥肠辘辘的他极度脱水，精疲力竭，就算放弃也完全在情理之中。

如果人们能够战胜这种情况，那么他们的脑海中一定有什么信念支撑着他们。许多人在遭遇类似的绝境时会选择放弃或精神失常，但幸存下来的人，靠的是心中的信念，是信念给予了他们战胜一切恶劣情况的勇气和决心。

"我跟自己说我一定可以挺过去的，"卡拉汉在他的叙述中写到。"跟别人的遭遇相比，我已经算是幸运的。我由始至终都这样鼓励自己，在自己心中建立起永不放弃的信念。"

读完这几句，我就把它们抄了下来，并深深地为之震撼。当我觉得自己的目标似乎遥不可及又或者我遇到了似乎无法解决的问题的时候，我就用它们来勉励自己。每每念及它们，我总能有所醒悟。

事实上，不幸都是相对而言的，有些人比我们更不幸。不管现实和理想相距多远，纵观历史，我们应该为现在所处的时代和境况感到幸运。这样的想法是明智的，而且也值得思考。

每一座山都有巅峰，每一个峡谷都有深底。人生也有兴衰起伏，不会有人一生都一帆风顺，也不会有人一生都时乖命蹇。难题总有了结的一天。随着时间的推移，一切难题都会迎刃而解。你也许不能控制时势，可是你能够冷静应对。你既可以把痛苦转换为怨天尤人的诅咒，也可以赋之以诗意，这全在于你自己的选择。

没有任何成功是不需要付出的，奋斗之后才会看到耀眼的阳光。人生的道路上有很多考验，需要我们坚持不懈，迎难而上。只要有一个信念在心中，再大的风浪都不能阻挡我们前进的步伐。在坚果与僵尸的战斗中，你需要一种战胜脆弱的精神，一种永不言败、自强不息的精神！不抛弃，不放弃！

温婉、平和的
睡莲

之一

睡莲篇
The Real Meaning of Peace

> Peace means to be in the midst of all those things and still be calm in your heart.
>
> 宁静是一种处乱不惊的内心祥和。

There once was a king who offered a prize to the artist who would paint the best picture of peace. Many artists tried. The king looked at all the pictures. But there were only two he really liked, and he had to choose between them.

One picture was of a calm lake. The lake was a perfect mirror for peaceful towering mountains all around it. Overhead was a blue sky with fluffy (松软的) white clouds. All who saw this picture thought that it was a perfect picture of peace.

The other picture had mountains, too. But these were rugged and bare. Above was an angry sky, from which rain fell and in which lightning played. Down the side of the mountain tumbled (翻滚) a foaming (起泡沫的) waterfall. This did not look peaceful at all.

But when the king looked closely, he saw behind the waterfall a tiny bush growing in a crack in the rock. In the bush a mother bird had built her nest. There, in the midst of the rush of angry water, sat the mother bird on her nest—in perfect peace.

Which picture do you think won the prize? The king chose the second picture. Do you know why?

"Because," explained the king, "peace does not mean to be in a place where there is no noise, trouble, or hard work. Peace means to be in the midst of all those things and still be calm in your heart. That is the real meaning of peace." (247 words)

(Extracted from "http://www.chinaenglish.com.cn/html/c61/2010-10/40896.html")

宁静的真谛

很久以前，有一个国王向画家们悬赏征集一幅最能表现宁静主题的画。画家们纷纷尝试。国王看完所有的画后，只挑中了两幅他真正喜欢的，他得在二者中选择其一。

第一幅画画的是一个平静的湖泊。水波不兴的湖面就像一面完美的镜子，倒映着四周屹然耸立的群山。湖的上方则是白丝绒般的云朵，飘浮于蔚蓝的苍穹。所有看到此画的人无不称赞其对宁静主题的完美体现。

另一幅画画的也是群山。但这些山却崎岖不平，寸草不生。群山上空是狂怒的天空，电闪雷鸣，暴雨倾盆。在山的一侧还有瀑布翻腾而下，撞击出白色的水沫。这幅画看来毫无安宁可言。

但是国王凝神细看的时候，却发现瀑布后面岩石的缝隙中有一小丛灌木，一只雌鸟已在灌木丛中筑好了自己的巢。在如此狂奔四泄的瀑布旁，雌鸟却安详地端坐巢中，完全没受到打扰。

你认为哪一幅赢得了赏金？国王选中了第二幅。知道是什么缘故吗？

"那是因为，"国王解释道："宁静并非意味着身处没有噪音、没有烦扰、毫无艰辛的环境之中。宁静是一种处乱不惊的内心祥和。这才是宁静的真谛。"

"植物大战僵尸"的战场上风云变幻、硝烟弥漫，有豌豆们的进攻，有玉米大炮的轰炸，但在这些轰轰烈烈的下面，都不能少了睡莲那平静的承载。睡莲以自己对宁静的解读构建了自己家园的攻守而最终胜利。像睡莲一样，其实宁静是一种关系，宁静是一种处乱不惊的内心祥和。这才是宁静的真谛。

睡莲篇
Right Beside You

> The gift of love can bring light where there is darkness.
>
> 这就是爱的礼物，它能给黑暗中的人带来光明。

The passengers on the bus watched sympathetically (同情地) as the young woman with the white cane made her way carefully up the steps. She paid the driver and then, using her hands to feel the location of the seats, settled into one. She placed her briefcase on her lap and rested her cane against her leg.

It had been a year since Susan, thirty-four, became blind. As the result of a medical accident she was sightless, suddenly thrown into a world of darkness, anger, frustration (挫折) and self-pity. All she had to cling (依靠) to was her husband Mark.

Mark was an Air Force officer and he loved Susan with all his heart. When she first lost her sight, he watched her sink into despair and he became determined to use every means possible to help his wife.

Finally, Susan felt ready to return to her job, but how would she get there? She used to take the bus, but she was now too frightened to get around the city by herself. Mark volunteered to ride the bus with Susan each morning and evening until she got the hang of it. And that is exactly what happened.

For two weeks, Mark, military uniform and all, accompanied Susan to and from work each day. He taught her how to rely on her other senses, specifically her hearing, to determine where she was and how to adapt to her new environment. He helped her befriend the bus drivers who could watch out for her, and save her a seat.

Each morning they made the journey together, and Mark would take a taxi back to his office. Although that meant he had to travel through the city and the routine was costly and exhausting, Mark knew it was only a matter of time before Susan would be able to ride the bus on her own. He believed in her.

Finally, Susan decided that she was ready to try the trip on her own. Monday morning arrived. Before she left, she embraced (拥抱) her husband tightly. Her eyes filled with tears of gratitude (感激) for his loyalty (忠诚), his patience, and his love. She said good-bye and, for the first time, they went their separate ways. Monday, Tuesday, Wednesday, Thursday... Each day on her own went perfectly, and a wild gaiety (欢乐) took hold of Susan. She was doing it! She was going to work all by herself!

On Friday morning, Susan took the bus to work as usual. As she was exiting the bus, the driver said, "Miss, I sure envy you." Curious, Susan asked the driver why.

"You know, every morning for the past week, a fine looking gentleman in a military uniform has been standing across the corner watching you when you get off the bus. He makes sure you cross the street safely and he watches you until you enter your office building. Then he blows you a kiss, gives you a salute and walks away. You are one lucky lady." the bus driver said.

Tears of happiness poured down Susan's cheeks. She was so lucky for he had given her a gift more powerful than sight, a gift she didn't need to see to believe—the gift of love that can bring light where there is darkness. (542 words)

就在你身边

译文

当这个手持白杖的年轻女子小心翼翼地上车时，车上的乘客都向她投去怜悯的目光。她向司机付了车费之后，双手摸索着座位，然后坐好，把公文包放在膝盖上，手杖靠着腿。

34岁的苏珊失明已有一年了。一起医疗事故夺去了她的视力，她顿时陷入黑暗之中，内心充满愤怒、沮丧，还有顾影自怜，而她可以依靠的只有她的丈夫马克了。

马克是名空军军官，他深爱着苏珊。苏珊失明的头些日子，他眼睁睁地看着妻子陷入绝望，心里打定主意，要尽一切办法帮助她。

后来，苏珊终于愿意重返工作岗位了。可她怎么去上班呢？以前都是乘公交车去的，但是她现在很害怕，不敢一个人在城里转。于是马克自告奋勇早晚坐公车接送她，直到她可以一个人应付。这就是事情的经过。

植物与僵尸

整整两周，马克每天都一身戎装，陪着苏珊一起上下班，教她怎么凭借其他感官，尤其是听觉，判断她所处的位置，以及如何适应新的环境。他还帮她与司机交好，这样司机就能照顾她，并给她留个座位。

每天早上，他们都一起同行，然后马克再乘出租车回去上班。尽管马克得穿过整座城市，而且疲惫不堪，又花费不菲，但是他坚信苏珊一定能独自乘车，这只是时间问题。他相信她。

最后，苏珊决定自己独自坐车上班。星期一上午，临行前，她紧紧地拥抱着自己的丈夫，眼里蓄满了感激的泪水，感谢他的忠诚，他的耐心，还有他的爱。她向他道了别，他们第一次朝着不同的方向走去。周一、周二、周三、周四……每天她的独行之旅都很顺利，苏珊感到一阵狂喜。她成功了！她真的能一个人去上班了！

周五早上，苏珊照常乘公共汽车去上班。就要下车了，司机说："小姐，我真羡慕你啊！"苏珊感到很奇怪，便问司机为什么。

"是这样的，这个星期，每天早上都有一个仪表堂堂、穿着军装的男士一直站在拐弯处看着你下车，看着你安全地穿过街道，又看着你走进办公楼，他给你个飞吻，冲你行个礼，然后才动身离去。你真是个幸运的姑娘啊！"司机说。

苏珊的脸上流下幸福的泪水。她是幸运的，因为马克给了她比视力更珍贵的礼物，一份她不需要看就能体会到的礼物——这就是爱的礼物，它能给黑暗中的人带来光明。

我们家园的池塘里能够承载植物的只有睡莲，它总是宁静地、默默地承载着一切。也许那些攻击性植物正为自己的炮火强烈沾沾自喜，也许那些防守性植物正在为自己的皮糙肉厚鼓掌欢庆，但正是睡莲无私的陪伴和承载铸就了它们的辉煌，这就是爱的呵护和礼物，它能给黑暗带来光明，它能化腐朽为神奇。

睡莲篇
Melodious Sound

> When Dad played his fiddle, the world became a bright star.
>
> 每当爸爸拉起小提琴，世界就变成一颗闪亮的星星。

When Dad played his fiddle (小提琴), the world became a bright star. To him violin was an instrument of faith, hope and charity. At least a thousand times, my mother said, "Your papa would play his fiddle if the world was about to blow up."

And once Dad came about as close to that as could ever be possible.

Everything on Nubbin Ridge — and on a majority of the small farms in Texas — was built around cotton as the money crop. But in the early years of the century, the boll weevil (棉籽象鼻虫) began devastating (破坏) the cotton farms in the south.

And in May of 1910 folks all over the nation were in a space-age state of turmoil (焦虑) over Halley's Comet. There were all sorts of frightening stories about the comet, the main one being that the world would pass through its tail, said to be millions of miles long.

Between the threats of comet and weevils, the farmers were running low on optimism. One night, the farmers gathered at our farm to discuss what to do. When everyone had found seats, Will Bowen suggested, "Charley, how about getting down your fiddle and bow and giving us a little music?"

"Aw, I don't think anybody would want to hear me saw the gourd (葫芦) tonight," Dad replied.

"Come on, Mr. Nordyke," one of the younger women urged, "why don't you play for us?"

Dad had a knack (本领) for getting people in the mood for his music. Knowing of the scattered prejudice against the fiddle, he eased into a song titled Gloryland. It was a church song with church tones, but it was fairly fast with some good runs. He shifted from Gloryland to The Bonnie Blue Flag, a Confederate war song, which created a big stir — foot stamping, hand clapping and a few rebel yells.

Will Bowen, apparently having forgotten Halley's Comet, shouted, "How about giving us Sally Goodin?" Dad played the old breakdown with vigor. Several men jumped up and jigged around. Children gathered around and gazed wide-eyed at the performance.

All our neighbors went home whistling or humming. Very few remembered to look toward the northwest to see whether the comet and its wicked tail were still around...

One evening, Will Bowen called dad on the telephone and said, "Charley, I'm downhearted and blue. Every time a square forms, there are four boll weevils waiting there to puncture (刺穿) it with their snouts. Just wondered if you could play a tune or two for me?"

"I sure could, Will," Dad said. "Could you come over?"

"No. I mean play on the phone box."

"The phone box?"

"Sure," Mr. Bowen said. "I can hear you talk. Why couldn't I hear the fiddle?"

Dad took the fiddle to the telephone and thumped (重击) the strings. Putting the receiver to his ear, he said, "Hear anything, Will?"

"Sure can," Mr. Bowen said. "Could you try Sally Goodin and

play it just like you did the other night?" Dad handed the receiver to me. He stepped up to the mouthpiece on the wall box and cut loose on Sally Goodin. I could bear Mr. Bowen whistling and yelling.

By the time the tune was finished there were half a dozen neighbors on the line, and they talked about how wonderful the music sounded over the telephone. They made numerous requests; I relayed them to Dad and he played the numbers.

Our party line broadcasts became regular features of community life. On rough-weather days of winter when farm folks were forced to remain in the house, someone would ring us and ask Dad to play, and usually it developed into a network affair. Our phone kept ringing with requests for music until radio came in. (617 words)

悠扬的琴声

译文

每当爸爸拉起小提琴，世界就变成一颗闪亮的星星。对爸爸来说，小提琴是一种能带来信念、希望和善意的乐器。妈妈曾不下一千次说过，"即使世界下一秒就要灰飞烟灭，你爸爸还是会拉他的小提琴。"

有一回，爸爸几近要面临那可能发生的一幕。

　　纽宾山以及德克萨斯州大部分的小农场的一切，都是建立在棉花这种经济作物上的。然而在上世纪初期，棉籽象鼻虫开始侵蚀美国南部的棉花农场。

　　1910年5月，全美国人民都处在太空时代的焦虑中，担心着哈雷彗星带来的危害。关于彗星骇人听闻的说法林林总总，传得最厉害的就是彗星的彗尾将扫过地球，据说彗尾长达数百万英里。

　　面对着彗星和象鼻虫的双重威胁，农场主们都忧心忡忡。一天晚上，农场主们聚集在我们的农场讨论该怎么办。大家纷纷落座后，威尔·鲍温建议："查理，把你的小提琴和琴弓拿出来，给大伙来点儿音乐怎么样？"

　　"噢，我觉得今晚没人想听我拉那葫芦吧。"爸爸回应道。

　　"来吧，诺达克先生，"一个年轻妇女催促说，"你就给我们拉一把吧！"

　　爸爸有这么一种能耐，能将大家带入他的音乐氛围中。知道有些人对拉小提琴存有异见，他先来了首《荣耀之地》暖场。这是一首教会的歌，有着教会的调式，但节奏较快，有几段精彩的急奏。然后，他从《荣耀之地》过渡到《美丽的蓝旗》——一首南北战争时南方联盟的战歌，这首歌在人群中引起了很大的共鸣，场上响起了踩脚声、打拍子声，还有喝彩声。

　　威尔·鲍温明显已经把哈雷彗星的事忘得一干二净了，嚷了起来，"来首《沙丽·古丁》怎么样？"爸爸又兴致勃勃地拉奏了这首经典的踩脚拽步舞曲。有几个人应声而起，跳起舞来了。孩子们也围拢过来专注地看着这段表演，眼睛都睁得大大的。

　　所有的邻居在回家时要么吹着口哨，要么就哼着曲儿。几乎没人还记得要看看那西北方是否还有哈雷彗星和它那邪恶的尾巴的踪迹……

　　一天晚上，威尔·鲍温给爸爸打来电话说，"查理，我很失落很担心。每长出一个棉蕾，就有四只象鼻虫蠢蠢欲动，等着用象鼻往里面钻。你能不能给我拉一两首曲子？"

　　"当然可以啦，威尔，"爸爸说，"你可以过来吗？"

　　"不，我的意思是在电话里拉。"

"在电话里？"

"是啊，"鲍温先生说，"我能听到你说话，怎么会听不到你的琴声呢？"

爸爸把小提琴拿到话机旁，重重地拨弄了几下琴弦。然后他把听筒拿到耳边，问："威尔，听得到吗？"

"当然听得到，"鲍温先生说，"你能不能拉《沙丽·古丁》，就像前几天那样？"爸爸把听筒递给我。他向前走近挂在墙上的话筒，尽情地拉奏起这首《沙丽·古丁》。我听到电话那头传来鲍温先生的口哨声和欢呼声。

曲终之时，电话的那头已经聚集了六位邻居，他们谈论着透过电话聆听音乐有多美妙。他们又点了很多曲子，我转告爸爸，他都一一演奏了。

我们的派对热线广播成为了当地生活的固定节目。当严冬季节将务农的人们困在室内的时候，就会有人给我们打电话，请爸爸给他们拉小提琴。久而久之，这慢慢成为了一种社交生活。在无线电广播普及之前，我们家的点播热线总是响个不停。

音乐的神奇远远不只是调节生活那么简单，对"音乐"我们"聆听"、"欣赏"或"享受"也仍显得苍白。音乐不能吃穿却可以改变生活，正如睡莲之于"植物大战僵尸"，睡莲不参与攻防，却是不可或缺的坚强后盾。每次游戏前玩家都要把睡莲放在装备栏中，有睡莲在植物们才会放心，因为睡莲是奇迹发生的地方。

睡莲篇
Find Something Beautiful to Notice

From now on, on your way to school, or on your way home, find something beautiful to notice.

从今以后，在上学的路上，或是在回家的路上，要发现一些美丽的事物。

A very special teacher in a high school had a husband who died suddenly of a heart attack. About a week after his death, she shared some of her thoughts with a classroom of students. On the late afternoon, sunlight shined through the classroom windows, and when the class was nearly over, she moved a few things aside on her desk and sat down there.

With a gentle look on her face, she paused and said, "Before class is over, I would like to share with all of you a thought which I feel is very important. Each of us is put here on earth to learn, share, love, appreciate (欣赏) and give of ourselves... and none of us knows when this fantastic (美好的) experience will end. It can be taken away at any moment. Perhaps this is a sign that we must make the most out of every single day."

Her eyes beginning to water, she went on, "So I would like you all to make me a promise... from now on, on your way to school, or on your way home, find something beautiful to notice. It doesn't have to be something you see — it could be a scent — perhaps of freshly baked bread wafting out of someone's house, or it could be the sound of the breeze slightly rustling (发出沙沙声) the leaves in the trees, or the way the morning light catches one autumn leaf as it falls gently to the ground. Please, look for these things, and remember them."

"For, although it may sound silly to some people, these things are the 'stuff' of life. The little things we are put here on earth to enjoy. The things we often take for granted. We must make it important to notice them, for at any time... they can all be taken away."

The class was completely quiet. We all picked up our books and filed out of the room silently. That afternoon, I noticed more things on my way home from school than I had that whole semester (学期).

Every once in a while, I think of that teacher and remember what an impression she made on all us, and I try to appreciate all of those things that sometimes we all overlook (忽略).

Take notice of something special you see on your lunch hour today. Go barefoot. Or walk on the beach at sunset. Stop off on the way home tonight to get a double dip ice-cream cone. For as we get older, it is not the things we did that we often regret, but the things we didn't do. (427 words)

(Extracted from "http://www.paedu.net/geyan/EnglishArticles/shuangyu/201003/43649.html")

译文

发现身边的美

一位很特别的高中老师，她的丈夫死于心脏病突发。在他死后大约一周，她便把她的一些所思所想讲给全班学生听。在那天下午，阳光透过教室的窗户照射进来，快要放学了，她把一些东西放在讲桌上，在那儿坐了下来。

她脸上带着温柔的表情，稍稍停顿了一下，说道，"在放学前，我想跟你们分享一种我认为很重要的想法。我们每个人都生活在地球上，学习、分享、关爱、欣赏和付出自我，却没有一个人知道这种美好的体验什么时候就会结束了。它随时都可能被带走。也许这预示着我们必须最大限度地利用每一个日子。"

她的眼睛湿润了，她继续说道，"因此我想让你们每个人答应我，从今以后，在你上学的路上，或者回家的路上，要发现一些美丽的事物。它不一定是你看到的某个东西——它可能是一种香味——也许是从谁的家里飘出来的新鲜烤面包的味道，也许是微风轻拂树叶的声音，或者是晨光照射在轻轻飘落的秋叶上的情景。请你们寻找这些东西并且记住它们吧。"

"因为，尽管这对有些人来说有些傻气，但这些东西就是生活的内容，是我们活在世上要欣赏的一些小东西。我们经常认为这些东西是理所当然的。但我们必须注意它们，这很重要，因为说不定在什么时候，它们就被带走了。"

整个教室里非常安静。我们都收拾起课本，一个个默默地走出教室。那天下午，在放学回家的路上我注意到很多事物，比我以前整个学期发现的事物还要多。

　　不时地，我会想到那位老师，回忆起她给我们留下的深刻印象，我便会尽力去欣赏有时我们都忽略的东西。

　　今天中午吃饭的时候注意一下你所看到的特别事物。光着脚丫散散步，或在日落时分在沙滩上漫步。今晚在回家的路上，要驻足仔细品味一下冰淇淋蛋卷。因为随着我们年龄的增长，让我们后悔的并不是做过的事情，而是那些没能去做的事情。

　　其实睡莲是有一双小眼睛的。难道，睡莲在炮火连天、硝烟弥漫的战场上还有时间看风景？我们也一样，于纷杂的工作和生活中也不要忽略身边那些美丽的事物。正如诗人泰戈尔所说：如果你因错过太阳而流泪，那么你也将错过群星（IF YOU SHED TEARS WHEN YOU MISS THE SUN, YOU ALSO MISS THE STARS.）。

‖温婉、平和的睡莲‖

之
五

睡莲篇

Be Still

Savor the stillness. It's a treasure, and it's available to us, always.

品味平静。它是财富，就在每个人身边，而且唾手可得。

Be still. Just for a moment.

Listen to the world around you. Feel your breath coming in and going out. Listen to your thoughts. See the details of your surroundings.

Be at peace with being still.

In this modern world, activity and movement are the default (默认的) modes, if not with our bodies then at least with our minds, with our attention. We rush around all day, doing things, talking, emailing, sending and reading messages, clicking from browser tab to the next, one link to the next.

We are always on, always connected, always thinking, always talking. There is no time for stillness — and sitting in front of a frenetic (忙乱的) computer all day, and then in front of the hyperactive (极度活跃的) television, doesn't count as stillness.

This comes at a cost: we lose that time for contemplation (沉思), for observing and listening. We lose peace.

And worse yet: all the rushing around is often counterproductive

(相反效果). I know, in our society action is all–important — inaction (无作为) is seen as lazy and passive and unproductive. However, sometimes too much action is worse than no action at all. You can run around crazily, all sound and fury, but get nothing done. Or you can get a lot done — but nothing important. Or you can hurt things with your actions, make things worse than if you'd stayed still.

And when we are forced to be still — because we're in line for something, or waiting at a doctor's appointment, or on a bus or train — we often get antsy (烦躁的), and need to find something else to do. Some of us will have our mobile devices, others will have a notebook or folder with things to do or read, others will fidget (坐立不安). Being still isn't something we're used to.

Take a moment to think about how you spend your days — at work, after work, getting ready for work, evenings and weekends. Are you constantly rushing around? Are you constantly reading and answering messages, checking on the news and the latest stream of information? Are you always trying to get lots of things done, ticking off tasks from your list like a machine, rushing through your schedule?

Is this how you want to spend your life?

If so, peace be with you. If not, take a moment to be still. Don't think about what you have to do, or what you've done already. Just be in the moment.

Then after a minute or two of doing that, contemplate your life, and how you'd like it to be. See your life with less movement, less doing, less rushing. See it with more stillness, more contemplation, more peace.

Then be that vision.

It's pretty simple, actually: all you have to do is sit still for a little bit each day. Once you've gotten used to that, try doing less each day. Breathe when you feel yourself moving too fast. Slow down. Be present. Find happiness now, in this moment, instead of waiting for it.

Savor the stillness. It's a treasure, and it's available to us, always. (502 words)

(Extracted from "http://zenhabits.net")

译
文

平静着

平静着。这样停留片刻。

细细聆听你周围的这个世界，感受自己的一呼一吸。倾听自己的思想，观察身边的每一个细节。

平静又平和着。

现今社会，活动和移动已是生活的常态，即使我们身体不动，意识也是在不停运转着。每天我们都四处奔忙，工作、谈话、发邮件、收发短信，从一个浏览器到另一个浏览器、从一个链接到另一个链接。

我们总是在忙，总是在联系、在思考、在谈论。没有时间平静。整天在电脑前一屁股坐下来就开始疯狂工作，回家后又继续坐着看电视，那不是真正意义上的平静。

为此我们付出了代价：没有时间去沉思、观察和聆听。我们失去了平和。

更糟的是，这种奔忙经常会带来相反的效果。据我所知，在这个社会，行动是最重要的——不行动会被认为是懒惰、消极、没有意义的表现。然而，有些时候行动过度比不行动还要糟。你疯狂地、愤怒地跑来跑去，到头来什么都没有得到；或者你得到了很多——但却没有一件是重要的；或者你的行动伤害到了某些东西，使事情更糟，还不如不做的好。

当我们被迫平静时——排队、看病挂号、等公交、等火车——我们常常急躁地想在这时再做点儿什么。一些人开始玩手机，还有的开始阅读文件，另外一些人在烦躁地等待。我们已经不能习惯静止的状态了。

花一些时间思考自己要怎样度过每一天——上班、工作、下班、晚上和周末。你是否一直在忙碌，一直在收发短信，查看新闻、追踪信息？你是不是总想赶着把事情做完，像机器一样完成计划栏里的任务？

这是你想要过的生活吗？

如果是这样的话，祝愿你一生平和。如果不是，请花时间让自己平静。不要想自己还有什么事情要做，或者已经做了哪些事。让自己平静下来。

在接下来的一两分钟里，审视一下自己的生活，你希望它怎样发展。让你的生活少一些活动、工作和忙碌，多一些思考、平静和平和。

然后去想象。

实际上，这个很简单：就是每天让自己平静一会儿。一旦习惯，便可以适当减少每日的工作强度。在感到自己节奏太快的时候做深呼吸。慢慢平静下来。活在当下。寻找身边即得的幸福，而不是等待它的到来。

品味平静。它是财富，就在每个人身边，而且唾手可得。

古人"每日三省吾身"，我们是否能花一些时间思考每一天的所得所失呢？睡莲似乎可以做到这些，不管"植物大战僵尸"的战场上如何硝烟弥漫，睡莲似乎都可以平静着，感受自己的一呼一吸，感受那战场外的桃源。也许整个游戏中，只有睡莲才能注意到我们家园真正的存在。

激情、有魄力
的辣椒

辣椒篇
Enthusiasm Takes You Further

> Nothing great was ever achieved without enthusiasm.
> 没有热情就不会有任何伟大的成就。

Years ago, when I started looking for my first job, wise advisers urged, "Barbara, be enthusiastic! Enthusiasm will take you further than any amount of experience." How right they were. Enthusiastic people can turn a boring drive into an adventure, extra work into opportunity and strangers into friends.

"Nothing great was ever achieved without enthusiasm." wrote Ralph Waldo Emerson. It is the paste that helps you hang in there when the going gets tough. It is the inner voice that whispers, "I can do it!" when others shout, "No, you can't."

It took years and years for the early work of Barbara McClintock, a geneticist who won the 1983 Nobel Prize in medicine, to be generally accepted. Yet she didn't let up on her experiments. Work was such a deep pleasure for her that she never thought of stopping.

We are all born with wide-eyed, enthusiastic wonder as anyone knows who has ever seen an infant's delight at the jingle of keys or the scurrying (急走) of a beetle.

It is this childlike wonder that gives enthusiastic people such a youthful air, whatever their age. At 90, cellist Pablo Casals would start his day by playing Bach. As the music flowed through his fingers, his stooped shoulders would straighten and joy would reappear in his eyes. Music, for Casals, was an elixir (长生不老药) that made life a never ending adventure. As author and poet Samuel Ullman once wrote, "Years wrinkle (长皱纹) the skin, but to give up enthusiasm wrinkles the soul."

How do you rediscover the enthusiasm of your childhood? The answer, I believe, lies in the word itself. "Enthusiasm" comes from the Greek and means "God within". And what is God within is but an abiding (持久的) sense of love — proper love of self (self-acceptance) and, from that, love of others.

Enthusiastic people also love what they do, regardless of money or title or power. If we can not do what we love as a full-time career, we can consider it as a part-time avocation (业余爱好), like the head of state who paints, the nun who runs marathons, the executive who handcrafts furniture.

Elizabeth Layton of Wellsville, Kan, was 68 before she began to draw. This activity ended bouts (一次) of depression that had plagued (折磨) her for at least 30 years, and the quality of her work led one critic to say, "I am tempted to call Layton a genius." Elizabeth has rediscovered her enthusiasm.

We can't afford to waste tears on "might-have-been". We need to turn the tears into sweat as we go after "what-can-be".

We need to live each moment wholeheartedly, with all our senses — finding pleasure in the fragrance (芳香) of a back-yard garden, the crayoned picture of a six-year-old, the enchanting beauty of a rainbow. It is such enthusiastic love of life that puts a sparkle in our eyes, a lilt in our steps and smooth the wrinkles from our souls. (479 words)

(Extracted from "http://www.for68.com/new/201112/qi1797435301912111025916.shtml")

热情成就未来

多年前，当我第一次找工作时，不少有识之士强烈向我建议，"芭芭拉，要有热情！热情比任何经验都更有益。"这话多么正确。热情的人可以把沉闷的旅途变成探险，把加班变成机会，把陌生人变成朋友。

"没有热情就不会有任何伟大的成就。"拉尔夫·沃尔多·爱默生写道。当事情进展不顺时，热情是帮助你坚持下去的黏合剂。当别人叫喊"你不行"时，热情是你发自内心的呼唤——我能行！

1983年诺贝尔医学奖的获得者、遗传学家芭芭拉·麦克林托克早年的工作直到很多年后才被公众所承认，但她并没有放弃实验。工作对她来说是一种如此巨大的快乐，她从未想过停止。

我们都生来好奇，睁大眼睛，满怀热情，每一个看到过婴儿听到钥匙声或看见乱爬的甲虫就兴奋不已的人，都会明白这一点。

不论年龄大小，正是这种孩子气的好奇给了热情的人们一种青春的气息。大提琴家帕布罗·卡萨尔斯在90岁时还坚持以拉巴赫的乐曲开始他的每一天。音乐从他的指间流出，他弯着的背挺直起来，欢乐再度溢满他的眼眸。音乐对卡萨尔斯来说，就是灵丹妙药，它使人生变成无止境的探索之旅。就像作家兼诗人塞缪尔·厄尔曼曾写过的："岁月使皮肤布满皱纹，但如果失去热情，便会使灵魂衰老。"

怎样才能找回孩提时代的热情呢？我相信答案就在"热情"这个词本身。"热情"一词源于希腊语，原意是"内在的上帝"。这里所说的"内在的上帝"不是别的，而是一种持久不变的爱——适度的自爱（自我接受），并推及他人。

热情的人们同样热爱他们所做的事，而不去考虑金钱、地位或者权力。如果我们不能把热爱的事作为正式职业，我们也可把它当做业余消遣，比如有的国家元首喜欢画画，有的修女参加马拉松长跑，有的行政官员手工制作家具。

堪萨斯州韦尔斯维尔市的伊丽莎白·莱顿到68岁才开始画画，这一爱好消除了曾纠缠她至少达30年之久的忧郁症，而她的作品水准之高使得一个评论家说："我忍不住要称莱顿为天才。"伊丽莎白又找回了她的热情。

我们不应该把眼泪浪费在"早该"之类的后悔上。我们需要把眼泪化为汗水，去追求"可能"的事情。

我们需要以全副身心去度过生命中的每一分钟——在后花园的芬芳中，在6岁小孩的蜡笔画中，在彩虹醉人的美中，找到快乐。正是这种对生活的热爱，让我们双目有神，让我们步履矫健，让我们的灵魂愈发年轻。

做事情没有智慧和才能是可怕的，但没有热情更可怕，冷漠和平淡就如一个一个僵尸正在慢慢侵蚀你的生命家园，"没有热情就不会有任何伟大的成就"，我们要像辣椒那样对周遭充满热情，烧毁那些沉闷的"僵尸"，用我们的热情把生命家园建设得更加绚丽！

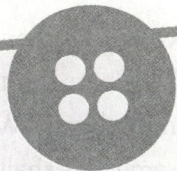

辣椒篇
Relish the Moment

> Life must be lived as we go along. The station will come soon enough.
>
> 生活得一边过一边瞧。车站就会很快到达。

Tucked away in our subconscious is an idyllic (田园风光的) vision. We see ourselves on a long trip that spans the continent. We are traveling by train. Out the windows, we drink in the passing scene of cars on nearby highways, of children waving at a crossing, of cattle grazing on a distant hillside, of smoke pouring from a power plant, of row upon row of corn and wheat, of flatlands and valleys, of mountains and rolling hillsides, of city skylines and village halls.

But uppermost (最重要的) in our minds is the final destination. On a certain day at a certain hour, we will pull into the station. Bands will be playing and flags waving. Once we get there, so many wonderful dreams will come true and the pieces of our lives will fit together like a completed jigsaw (拼图) puzzle. How restlessly we pace the aisles, damning the minutes for loitering (游荡) — waiting, waiting, waiting for the station.

"When we reach the station, that will be it!" we cry. "When I'm 18." "When I buy a new 450SL Mercedes Benz!" "When I put the last kid through college." "When I have paid off the mortgage!" "When I get a promotion." "When I reach the age of retirement, I shall live happily ever after!"

Sooner or later, we must realize there is no station, no one place to arrive at once and for all. The true joy of life is the trip. The station is only a dream. It constantly outdistances us.

"Relish the moment" is a good motto, especially when coupled with Psalm 118: 24: "This is the day which the Lord hath made; we will rejoice (欣喜) and be glad in it." It isn't the burdens of today that drive men mad. It is the regrets over yesterday and the fear of tomorrow. Regret and fear are twin thieves who rob us of today.

So stop pacing the aisles and counting the miles. Instead, climb more mountains, eat more ice cream, go barefoot more often, swim more rivers, watch more sunsets, laugh more, cry less. Life must be lived as we go along. The station will come soon enough. (359 words)

(Extracted from "http://www.tingvoa.com/html/20110905/52987.html")

享受此刻

　　我们的潜意识里藏着一派田园诗般的风光。

　　我们仿佛身处一次横贯大陆的漫漫旅程之中。乘着火车，我们领略着窗外流动的景色：附近高速公路上奔驰的汽车、十字路口处招手的孩童、远山上吃草的牛群、源源不断地从电厂排放出的烟尘、一片片的玉米和小麦、平原与山谷、群山与绵延的丘陵、天空映衬下城市的轮廓，以及乡间的庄园宅第。

然而我们心里想得最多的却是最终的目的地。在某一天的某一时刻，我们将会抵达进站，迎接我们的将是乐队和飘舞的彩旗。一旦到了那儿，多少美梦将成为现实，我们的生活也将变得完整，如同一块理好了的拼图。可是我们现在在过道里不耐烦地踱来踱去，咒骂火车的拖拖拉拉。我们期待着，期待着，期待着火车进站的那一刻。

"当我们到站的时候，一切就都好了！"我们呼喊着。"当我18岁的时候！""当我有了一辆新450SL奔驰的时候！""当我供最小的孩子念完大学的时候！""当我偿清贷款的时候！""当我官升高任的时候！""当我到了退休的时候，就可以从此过上幸福的生活啦！"

可是我们终究会认识到人生的旅途中并没有车站，也没有能够"一到永逸"的地方。生活的真正乐趣在于旅行的过程，而车站不过是个梦，它始终遥遥领先于我们。

"享受此刻"是句很好的箴言，尤其是当它与《圣经·诗篇》中第118页24行的一段话相呼应的时候，更是如此："今日乃主所创造；生活在今日我们将欢欣、愉悦！"真正令人发疯的不是今日的负担，而是对昨日的悔恨及对明日的恐惧。悔恨与恐惧是一对孪生窃贼，将今天从你我身边偷走。

那么就不要在过道里徘徊吧，别老惦记着你离车站还有多远！何不换一种活法，多爬爬山，多吃点儿冰淇淋，多光着脚板儿溜达溜达，多在河中畅游，多看看夕阳西下，多点儿欢笑，少些泪水！生活得一边过一边瞧。车站就会很快到达。

"植物大战僵尸"中，大多植物都是以种植为前提的，只有少数几种植物出场就会带来立竿见影的效果，出场即可烧毁一条直线僵尸的辣椒便是其中之一。我们常常或活在过去时里沉溺往事无法自拔，或活在将来时里无限憧憬，却很少有人能够把握住现在。学学干脆的辣椒吧，活在当下，拥有今天！

辣椒篇

The Recipe for Student Success—Real Passion

> Real Passion is magical. It creates motivation, determination and perseverance.
>
> 激情是一种神奇的东西，它给人以动力，决心和毅力。

"If there is no passion in your life, then have you really lived? Find your passion, whatever it may be. Become it, and let it become you and you will find great things happen for you, to you and because of you."

T. Alan Armstrong

There's no denying that going to college can get pretty expensive, not only in money but also in time. Firstly, there is the initial debt that comes from paying for tuition and accommodation, and then there's the time we lose having to work to pay it back. Going to university is a huge sacrifice, the question is, is it worth it?

The answer, I think, is yes, if you possess what is one of the most important ingredients in student success — Real Passion.

Real Passion is magical. It creates motivation, determination and perseverance. It gets you up in the morning, it energizes your day and it pushes you to the best of your ability.

In an ideal world, everyone would love the subject they're studying. There may or may not be other reasons for choosing it, but the main reason is that they want to learn. Now, this may seem obvious but up until now, I've met too many people that have forgotten the reason why they came to university. They spend too many nights out, they skip lectures and cram in all the work in at the last minute. They've forgotten their purpose, which is very sad, especially when I see it happening to my friends, the people that I have really come to care about. Of course, I myself am not perfect, and every now and again I have a lazy night in when I don't do a shred of work but eventually, I find my way back on track by finding my Real Passion.

What is Real Passion? This can be answered by asking what Unreal Passion is. Unreal Passion is lust, it's based on fickle things like beauty or money and it eventually burns out. If you're doing a subject because of salaries and titles, your happiness won't last. Real Passion means putting genuine love into everything you do, even if people tell you it's stupid and it doesn't pay well. It may not always be practical but as they say, "Do what you love and the money will follow."

Passion has many meanings, but the most crucial part of any kind of passion is desire. It may not be very "Zhen" of me to say it, but this kind of "desire" is different. Here, it is the desire to quench an unquenchable thirst for knowledge, a desire to do the best that we can and a desire to be happy.

I know it isn't always rainbows and butterflies, sometimes academic life is tough, and full of rough patches. But that's ok, as long as deep down inside the passion is still there, then you can keep going. (489 words)

(Extracted from "http://minimalstudent.com")

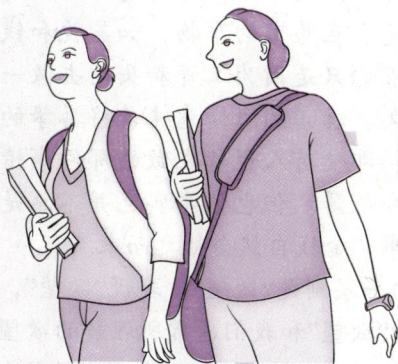

成功学生的
秘诀——激情

> "要是生活中没有激情，你算是真正的活过吗？寻找你的激情所在，让激情成为你生命中的一部分，你便会发现生活中会因你而发生很多意想不到的事情。"

> T·艾伦·阿姆斯特朗

毫无疑问，上大学既昂贵又费时。首先你就得支付学费和住宿费。另外，我们耗费了时间，其中的机会成本只有等我们工作以后才能赚回来。上大学要做不小的牺牲，而问题就在于，上大学值得这样的牺牲吗？

我的答案是肯定的。前提是你要对大学生活充满激情，这也是成功学生最重要的要素之一。

激情是神奇的，它给人以动力，决心和毅力。它使你一早醒来便能翻身而起，使你一天都充满活力，也使你能够最大限度地发挥自己。

在理想的情况下，每个人都喜欢自己所学的学科，也可能有其他的原因，但主要的原因就是他们自己愿意学，这点应该是显而易见的。但到目前为止，我遇到过很多人，他们都忘记了自己来大学上学的原因。他们在外出过夜、逃课、临时抱佛脚上面花费了非常多的时间，这很可悲，因为他们忘记了自己来大学的目的。而当这些事情发生在我的朋友，那些我真正关心的人身上的时候，我觉得更加伤心。当然，我自己也不是完人，我也时不时将一整夜都荒废掉，什么也不做。但我最后还是回到了正轨，找到了我真正的激情所在。

　　什么是真正的激情？要回答这个问题你只用弄清楚哪种激情是虚假的。虚假的激情是贪欲，它建立在易变的事物，如美貌和钱财的基础上，最终是会消失的。如果你只是因为工资和头衔去做一项学术研究的话，你的快乐不会持久。真正的激情意味着将真挚的爱投入到你所做的每件事情当中去，即使有人说你在做的那件事情有多么愚蠢，即使那件事情报酬十分微薄。但也许事实也并不总是这样，有个说法是，"做你所热爱的事，金钱自然会随之而来。"

　　激情有多层含义，但最重要的一层则是"欲望"。我说"欲望"，你也许觉得我不够清净无为，但这种"欲望"和我们通常所理解的欲望是不同的。这里的"欲望"是指你想去满足你对知识永不熄灭的渴求，想去追求卓越，想去追求幸福与快乐。

　　我知道学习的道路并不总是一帆风顺，有时候学术道路是艰难的，崎岖的。但是只要我们内心还充满着激情，我们便有力量继续前行。

　　"植物大战僵尸"中，辣椒绝对是最火辣的一个。它的火辣正像我们对某事的激情，是一种神奇的东西，它给人以动力、决心和毅力。真正拥有了激情，我们生活和事业中那些时间上、金钱上和知识上的困难，就会像僵尸一样在辣椒般的激情前荡然无存，我们的家园也会在激情的指引下愈发美丽、富饶。

辣椒篇
For God's Sake, Follow Your Dreams

Don't be scared to follow your dreams. That's the worst thing you can do to yourself.

不要害怕去实现自己的梦想。这将是你犯的最大的错误。

We all had some crazy ideas and dreams when we were kids. When people asked, "What do you want to do when you grow up?" You didn't say, "I want to play safe and be an executive for a Fortune 100 company" or "I want to work for the government for the job security." You wanted to do something that excited you, that you were passionate (激情的) about, "armed forces, scientist, sports, music, dance, Miss World" etc. You didn't even think if that would get you enough money. You just wanted to do it.

So why is it that as we grow up we lose all the passion, the energy, the will and the strength to keep our dreams alive? Why does money dictate our passion or in most cases, kill it? Why do we let "safety of a paycheck" screw our dreams? Why do we stop thinking about what we love?

We are so seduced (诱惑) by the thought of a guaranteed (保证) paycheck every month that we completely ignore the fact that it's actually never too late to pursue our dreams. The reason as I can understand is probably "fear of failure". We fear we might fail and that fear leads us to cook up stories about why you can't have what you want. Alibis like "I don't have time, I have family, I'll do it when I have more money etc". Stories that convince us that it's ok not to follow up on our dreams, that it's ok not to do what you love, that it's ok to just keep doing the everyday drill.

Like Tony Robbins puts it, "The only thing that's keeping you from getting what you want is the story you keep telling yourself about why you can't have it."

What are we waiting for? A perfect day when all stars would line up in just the right direction and you would be guaranteed success? It never works that way. That moment of glory never arrives. All circumstances will almost never be in your favor. There will always be something that would be challenging. You just have to bite the bullet and take the plunge (骤降). When we set out to create Rootein, we didn't wait for everything to be just perfect, much as we would have liked. We just dived in. We started developing Rootein while we were working full-time. We loved what we were doing and we did it while keeping our day time jobs. It wasn't easy, but it was fun because we were chasing our dream of working for ourselves, building software that we were passionate about.

Maybe it's just us. Maybe we are weird (奇怪的). Maybe we are foolish, but we would rather be foolish and strive (奋斗) to live our dream than come up with some alibis (借口). True success is not money-driven, it's driven by love and passion. You've got to love what you are doing and you've got to be passionate about it.

Failing is not scary. What's scary is that you are 60 and reflecting back on your life "Maybe I should've given my dreams a chance, maybe I would've succeeded, maybe I would've lived my dream." But now it's too late. You might have missed the boat.

Don't be scared to follow your dreams. That's the worst thing

you can do to yourself. (562 words)

不要放弃你的梦想

当还是小孩子的时候，我们都有过疯狂的主意和梦想。当人们问起："你长大后想干什么？"时，你不会说"我想做一份稳定的工作，我想在一家财富100强的公司里当总经理。"或者"我想在政府部门里找个铁饭碗。"你希望去做一些能让你兴奋的事情，你有热情的事情——"军人、科学家、运动员、音乐家、舞蹈家、世界小姐"等等。你根本不会考虑能从中获取多少钱，你只是想去做这些。

可是为什么长大后我们就失去了所有的热情、动力、愿望以及守住我们的梦想的力量了呢？为什么金钱就支配了我们的热情，大多数情况是扼杀了热情？为什么"一份稳定的收入"就能禁锢我们的梦想？为什么我们要停止思考我们热爱的事情？

我们受每月稳定工作收入的诱惑，以至于完全忽视了一个真相：追求自己的梦想永远不会太迟。我可以理解人们为什么会这样，人们是"害怕失败"。我们担心失败，这种担心导致了我们给自己编织了一个谎言：有些东西永远是不属于你的。"我没有时间，我有家庭，当我有了足够的钱后我会去做的，等等，"这些都是借口。这样我们就默认了丢掉梦想也没什么，不去做那些你热爱的事情也没什么，日复一日的做那些重复的枯燥的事情也没什么。

就像托尼·罗宾斯说的："唯一阻挡你去获取你想要的东西的事情是你一直在告诉自己为什么你无法拥有它。"

我们在等待什么？当所有的星星都能按你希望的方向连成一线的时刻吗？这样就能保证你一定成功吗？这条路永远是行不通的。这个光辉的时刻永远也不会到来。不会各种条件都尽如人意，永远都会有某方面的事情向你提出挑战。你不得不横下一条心、冒一回险。当我们开始创立Rootein网站的时候，我们不可能等待各方面都完美的时机、各方面都如我们所期待的那种情况出现。我们需要的是着手去做。我们在全职工作之余慢慢地发展这个网站。我们很喜欢现在所做的事情，而且我们也是做完我们白天的正式工作后做这些的。这不容易，但很有意思，因为我们正在实现我们的梦想，我们对正在开发的软件充满热情。

也许只有我们是这样想的，也许我们是怪人。也许我们很傻，但我们宁愿犯傻，宁愿活在梦想里拼搏，也不要找出一堆的借口。金钱的利诱不会带来真正的成功，真正的成功来自于爱和热情。你必须爱你所做的事情，你必须对你所做的事有热情。

失败并不可怕。可怕的是当你60岁时回首往事才发现"也许我应该给自己一次实现梦想的机会，也许我会成功的，也许我应该守住梦想。"但此时已经太晚了。你也许已经错过了时机。

不要害怕去实现自己的梦想。这将是你犯的最大的错误。

梦想面前，总有这样那样的困难如同一排排僵尸盘桓在我们实现梦想的路上，请不要放弃，总有些东西会像辣椒那样从天而降烧毁这些荆棘，比如我们的热情、我们的激情、我们坚定不移的信念，我们不折不挠的坚韧。不要放弃你的梦想，奇迹总会发生。

辣椒篇
I Am the Fire Goddess

> It was time to live my imagination not my history.
> 那一瞬间，我忘记了往昔，想象再次苏醒了。

When I was eight years old, I saw a movie about a mysterious island that had an erupting (喷发的) volcano and lush jungles filled with wild animals and cannibals (食人者). The island was ruled by a beautiful woman called Tondalaya, the Fire Goddess of the Volcano. It was a terrible low budget movie, but to me, it represented the perfect life. I desperately wanted to be the Fire Goddess. I wrote it on my list of things to be when I grow up.

Through the years, Tondalaya was forgotten. I spent the next 25 years being a good wife, eventually the mother of four, and a very respectable responsible member of society. My life was as bland and boring as a bowl of oatmeal.

The week I turned 50, my marriage came to a sudden end. I'd lost everything except my four teenage children. I had enough money to rent a cheap apartment while I looked for a job or I could use every penny I had to buy five plane tickets from Missouri to the most remote island in the world, the big island of Hawaii. Everyone said I was crazy to think I could just run off to an island and survive. They predicted (预测) I'd come crawling (爬行) back in a month. Part of me was afraid they were right.

The next day, my four children and I landed on the big island of Hawaii with less than $2,000, knowing no one in the world was going to help us. I worked 18 hours a day and lost 30 pounds because I lived on one meal a day. I had panic attacks that left me curled into a knot on the bathroom floor shaking like a shell-shocked soldier.

One night as I walked alone on the beach, I saw the red orange glow of the lava pouring out of Kilauea Volcano in the distance. I was wading in the Pacific Ocean, watching the world's most active volcano, and wasting that incredible moment, because I was haunted by the past, exhausted by the present and terrified of the future. I'd almost achieved my childhood dream but hadn't realized it, because I was focused on my burdens instead of my blessings. It was time to live my imagination not my history. Tondalaya, the Fire Goddess of the Volcano had finally arrived.

The next day, I quit my jobs and invested my last paycheck in art supplies and began doing what I loved. I hadn't painted a picture in 15 years, because we barely scratched out a living on the farm in Missouri, and there hadn't been money for the tubes of paint, and canvas (画布) and frames. I wondered if I could still paint or if I had forgotten how. My hands trembled the first time I picked up a brush. But before an hour had passed, I was lost in the colors spreading across the canvas in front of me. I painted pictures of old sailing ships and as soon as I started believing in myself, other people started believing in me, too. The first painting sold for $1,500 before I even had time to frame it.

The past six years have been filled with adventures. My children and I have gone swimming with dolphins, watched whales and hiked around the crater rim (火山口边缘) of the volcano. We wake up every morning with the ocean in front of us and the volcano behind us. The dream I had more than 40 years ago is now reality. I live on an island with a continuously erupting volcano. The only animals in the jungle are wild boars and mongooses (猫鼬) and there aren't any cannibals. But often in the evening, I can hear the drums from native dancers on the beach.

I'm free for the first time in my life. I am Tondalaya, the Fire Goddess of the Volcano. (642 words)

(Extracted from "http://www.24en.com/read/digest/2010-05-20/117562.html")

我就是火女神

八岁的时候，我看了一部电影：在神秘的岛屿上有一座喷发的火山和葱茏的丛林，丛林里到处是野生动物与食人族。统治岛屿的美丽女子是火山的火女神，名叫形达拉雅。那是部糟糕的低成本电影，然而对我而言，它表现了完美的人生。我极度渴望成为火女神。我将此列入长大之后要成为的人的清单中。

多年过去，我忘记了形达拉雅。随后25年我成为一名好妻子，四个孩子的母亲，可敬而负责的社会一员。生活平静乏味得像碗燕麦粥。

在我50岁的那个星期，我的婚姻突然结束了。除了我四个年少的孩子，我失去了一切。我的钱够用来在找工作的同时租一所廉价公寓，或者我可以倾尽积蓄买五张机票从密苏里飞往最遥远的岛屿——夏威夷的大岛。人人都认为我打算逃到一个岛上还认为能够活下去的想法太荒唐了。他们预测一个月后，我准会爬着回来。我隐隐地害怕他们是对的。

次日，四个孩子与我登上夏威夷的大岛，带的钱不足两千美元，我明白这世界上没人能够帮助我们。我每天工作18个小时，由于一天只吃一顿，体重下降了30磅。焦虑侵袭着我，我蜷曲在浴室的地板上，抖得像个患了炮弹震荡症的士兵。

　　一天夜晚，我走在沙滩上，看到远处乞劳伊阿火山喷出橙红色的岩浆。我正在太平洋沿岸趟水，观看着世界上最活跃的火山，然而我却白白地浪费了这精彩的一刻，因为过去让我挂怀，现在让我疲惫，而未来又让我惧怕。我只看到重担而没看到幸福，所以毫没意识到自己几乎已经实现了童年的梦想。那一瞬间，我忘记了往昔，想象再次苏醒了！形达拉雅——火山的火女神——终于到来了。

　　第二天，我辞去工作，把最后一笔薪水全花在艺术用品上，开始做起自己喜欢的事情来。15年以来我不曾画过一张画，因为在密苏里农场我们只是勉强糊口谋生，哪里还有钱买颜料、画布和画框。我怀疑自己是否还能画，怀疑自己是否还记得怎么画。第一次拿起画笔时，我的手都颤抖起来。还没到一个钟头，我就给涂在面前画布上的色彩弄得不知所措起来。我画的是古老的船只，等我渐渐拾起自信时，别人也开始对我有了信心。第一张画我还没来得及装框就卖出了1500美元。

　　过去的六年充满了冒险经历。孩子们与我和海豚一起游泳，观看鲸鱼，攀登火山口。每天早晨醒来，我们的前方是大海，后方是火山。我40多年前的梦想如今化为现实。我居住的岛上火山不断喷发，森林中只有野猪、猫鼬，没有食人族。而傍晚时分，我常常能听到土著人在海滩上跳舞的鼓声。

　　有生以来我第一次感到如此自由自在。我就是形达拉雅，火山之火女神。

　　曾经，在我们还小的时候，都有一个梦想。但是现实和梦想是有距离的，往往等我们长大后，我们都没去追逐我们的梦想，让梦想成为遗憾。看看我们可爱的辣椒吧！不管周遭多少僵尸蹒跚，辣椒都会开心地绽放，因为它有对梦想的坚信、执着和热情，因此梦想终究会属于它。

和平、正直的
三叶草

三叶草篇
An Invisible Smile

Smiles are contagious!
笑容是可以相互感染的!

Mr. Dawson was an old grouch (不高兴的人), and everyone in town knew it. Kids knew not to go into his yard to pick a delicious apple, even off the ground, because old Dawson, they said, would come after you with his ball bullet gun.

One Friday, 12-year-old Janet was going to stay all night with her friend Amy. They had to walk by Dawson's house on the way to Amy's house, but as they got close Janet saw him sitting on his front porch and suggested they cross over to the other side of the street. Like most of the children, she was scared of the old man because of the stories she'd heard about him.

Amy told her not to worry, Mr. Dawson wouldn't hurt anyone. Still, Janet was growing more nervous with each step closer to the old man's house. When they got close enough, Dawson looked up with his usual frown, but when he saw it was Amy, a broad smile changed his entire face as he said, "Hello, Miss Amy. I see you've got a little friend with you today."

Amy smiled back and told him Janet was staying overnight and they were going to listen to music and play games. Dawson told them that sounded fun, and offered them each a fresh picked apple off his tree. They gladly accepted. Dawson had the best apples in town.

When they got out of Dawson on earshot (听力所及之范围), Janet asked Amy, "Everyone says he's the meanest man in town. How come was he so nice to us?"

Amy explained that when she first started walking past his house, he wasn't very friendly and she was afraid of him, but she pretended (假装)he was wearing an invisible (不可见的)smile and so she always smiled back at him. It took a while, but one day he half-smiled back at her.

After some more time, he started smiling real smiles and then started talking to her. Just a "hello" at first, then more. She said he always offers her an apple now, and is always very kind.

"An invisible smile?" questioned Janet.

"Yes," answered Amy, "my grandma told me that if I pretended I wasn't afraid and pretended he was smiling an invisible smile at me and I smiled back at him, that sooner or later he would really smile. Grandma says smiles are contagious (感染性的；会蔓延的)."

If we remember what Amy's grandma said, that everyone wears an invisible smile, we will find that most people can't resist our smile after a while.

We're always on the go trying to accomplish (完成) so much, aren't we? Getting groceries, cleaning the house, mowing the lawn — there's always something. It's so easy to get caught up in everyday life that we forget how simple it can be to bring cheer to ourselves and others. Giving a smile away takes so little effort and time, let's make sure that we're not the one that others have to pretend is wearing an invisible smile. (495 words)

译文

看不见的微笑

道森先生是个脾气很坏的老头子，镇上的每个人都知道。就连小孩们都知道不能到他的院子里摘好吃的苹果，甚至掉在地上的也不能捡，据说，老道森会端着他的弹丸猎枪跟在后面追。

一个周五，12岁的珍妮特和她的朋友艾米度过一整夜。她们去艾米家的途中必须得路过道森先生的房子。当她们越来越接近道森家时，珍妮特看见道森先生坐在前廊，于是她提议她们过马路绕开道森家从街的另一边走。跟大多数孩子一样，珍妮特知道老道森的故事，很是害怕他。

艾米说别担心，道森先生不会伤害任何人。但每向前走一步，离老道森的房子越近，珍妮特就越紧张。当她们走近房子那儿时，道森抬起了头，一如既往地紧皱着眉头。但当他看到是艾米，一个灿烂的笑容改变了他的整个表情，他说："你好，艾米小姐，我看见今天有位小朋友陪你。"

艾米也对他微笑，告诉他珍妮特会整晚和她在一起，她们要一起听音乐、玩游戏。道森告诉她们这听上去很有趣，给她们每人一个从他院子里的树上刚摘下来的苹果。她们很高兴地接受了，因为道森的苹果是镇上最棒的。

走到道森听不到的地方，珍妮特问艾米："每个人都说他是镇上最不好相处的人，但他为什么会对我们这么好呢？"

艾米解释到，当她第一次路过他家时，他不是很友好，这让她

90

很害怕。但她假装他有着看不见的微笑，所以她总对他回之以微笑。终于过了一段时间，有一天，他也对她回以微笑。

再过了些日子，他开始真正地对她笑了，并开始和艾米说话。开始只是招呼一声，后来越来越多。她说他现在总给她苹果，总是很友善。

"看不见的笑容？"珍妮特问。

"是的，"艾米回答道。"我奶奶告诉我如果我假装不害怕，假装他有着看不见的笑容，我对他微笑，迟早有一天他会真正微笑起来。奶奶说笑容是可以互相感染的。"

如果我们记住艾米奶奶说的，相信每个人都有着看不见的笑容，我们会发现大多数人在一段时间后是无法抗拒我们的微笑的。

我们总是忙着去尽量完成更多的事，不是吗？买东西，打扫屋子，割院子里的草——总在忙碌着什么事。这就使我们很容易在日常生活中忘记：给自己和别人带来快乐是多么简单的事情。绽放微笑花费的精力与时间则更少。让我们确定自己不会成为这样的人——别人总得假装我们有着看不见的笑容。

僵尸的武器有时会蒙蔽我们的双眼，让我们分辨不出真实的样子。面对大家都十分惧怕的老者道森，小朋友艾米用自己的微笑使得道森敞开了心扉，使得他严肃的表情踪影全无。就好像三叶草面对无比强大的僵尸时，用无形的微笑迫使僵尸调头。敞开心扉，留住信任。绽放微笑，迎接和平。

三叶草篇
The Other Side of the Coin

I will give you a cadeau.

我给你一个礼物。

I was doing a big clean-up in the early part of last year and my kids were helping. As he rummaged (检查，搜出) through boxes and bags, one of my sons came across a knotted (打结的) handkerchief with an old dark brown coin nestled (半隐半现地处于) inside. "Mum, can I have this? Can I play with this in my cash register?" he asked. I took one look and was immediately transported to another time. "You can play with all your coins, but not this one," I said slowly. "This one is special. I will never again see the woman who gave this to me." I fingered the coin gently. "This coin is worth much more than its monetary (货币的) value."

My son looked at me strangely and I explained. In 1991, I had spent five months in a bleak (荒凉的) African country, Niger, ravaged (毁坏) by sandstorms and blistering (猛烈地) heat. There were many things I found difficult about this place — the climate and beggars were my biggest and most constant gripes (抱怨). Street urchins (顽童) would continually thrust their hands into your face, shouting "Cadeau! Cadeau!" [gift] in French, the former colonial tongue.

After I'd finished my nursing stint there, a friend and I headed for neighboring Burkina Faso to work in a health clinic.

"It's much greener in Burkina. Even the Coke tastes better." the locals assured us.

Arriving by taxi at our destination in Burkina, we began to unload. I had a large backpack and a smaller daypack (背包). With my daypack wedged between my legs, I reached for my larger piece of luggage. Out of the darkness, a motorbike with two men approached slowly. Without warning, one of the men grabbed my daypack as the motorbike swept close by. Within seconds, the two were out of sight, swallowed up by the night.

The bag had my passport, money, traveler's checks, camera, an airline ticket and other paraphernalia (随身用品) precious to me. I was in deep trouble. And the nearest Australian consulate (领事馆) was in Ethiopia.

In the weeks that followed, I zealously guarded the rest of my valuables and regarded all locals with suspicion. I endured interrogations (询问) by the authorities with thinly veiled frustration. All I wanted was to leave this hellhole. Then, walking through Burkina's streets one day, I was accosted by an old woman who thrusted her hand in my face. "Cadeau! Cadeau!" she cried.

I'd had enough. I was sick and tired of the country: its poverty and corruption (腐败), its thieves, its inefficiency, the heat, the dust and its time−wasting officials. I told her firmly in French, "I have no cadeau. I have no money. A thief stole all my money two weeks ago and now I can't get out of your country. I cannot give you anything."

The beggar woman listened attentively and pondered my words. Then her face crumpled (弄皱的) into a toothless grin as she reached into the folds of her dress.

"Then I will give you a cadeau," she announced. Kindly,

she placed an old, dark brown coin in my palm. I looked at it in shock. It was a minuscule (极小的) amount of money — but for this woman, the coin represented a meal. In that moment, I felt the shame of affluence and the humility of charity. She had given me a gift disproportionate (不成比例的) to anything that I had ever donated. In the midst of her poverty, she was able to give me something priceless.

I saw then the unexpected beauty of the people of Burkina Faso — and appreciated profoundly the quiet dignity of the poor. Humbled by the old woman's gift, I hope never to part with the coin she gave me. With one small token, she turned my perceptions upside down. (610 words)

(Extracted from "http://www.paedu.net/geyan/EnglishArticles/shuangyu/201002/43501_2.html")

硬币的另一面

去年早些时候我进行了一次大扫除，我的孩子们一起帮忙。我的一个儿子翻箱倒柜，发现一条打结的手帕，里面有一枚发黑的硬币。他问道："妈妈，可以给我吗？我想用它来玩收银机游戏。"我看了一眼，马上想起了另一段时光。"你可以玩我所有的硬币，但这枚不行，"我缓缓地说，"它很特殊。我再也不会碰见给我这枚硬币的女人了，"我抚摸着硬币，说道："这枚硬币的价值远远大于它本身的币值。"

我儿子奇怪地看着我，于是我解释给他听。1991年我在尼日尔呆了五个月。那是个荒凉的非洲国家，沙暴遍地，酷热难当。我最恨最烦的两件事就是天气和乞丐。流浪儿们时不时地把手伸到你面前，用法语喊着："礼物！礼物！"

护理工作结束之后，我和一位朋友去了邻国布基纳法索的一家健康中心工作。

当地人告诉我："布基纳法索比这里干净多了，就连可乐的味道都好得多。"

乘出租到达目的地后，我们开始卸行李。我有两个背包，一大一小。我把小包夹在双腿中间，去拿大包。黑暗中，两个男人骑着摩托车慢慢地靠近。当摩托车驶过的时候，其中一个男人突然抢走了我的小包。很快，两个人消失在夜色之中。

小包里有我的护照、钱、旅行支票、相机、机票和其他珍贵的私人物品。我的麻烦大了，最近的澳大利亚领事馆在埃塞俄比亚！

接下来的几个星期里，我警惕地保护着剩下的东西，怀疑每一个当地人，对当地部门的盘问也很不合作。我想的就是离开这个鬼地方。

一天，我走在布基纳法索的街上，碰到了一个老女人。她把手伸到我的面前，叫道："礼物！礼物！"

我受够了！我再也不能忍受这个国家，她的贫穷和腐败，她的小偷、无能、酷热、沙尘和浪费时间的官员。我直接用法语对她说："我没有礼物，没有钱。两个星期前，一个贼偷光了我的钱，搞得我现在没法离开你们的国家。我什么都给不了你。"

那个女乞丐仔细听着，琢磨着我的话。然后她咧嘴笑了，露出没牙的嘴巴，把手伸进了衣服的褶缝里。

"那么，我给你一个礼物。"她轻轻地把一枚发黑的硬币放在我手里。我吃惊地看着硬币，它的面额很低——但对那个女人而言，这就是一顿饭！那一刻，我感到无地自容。她给我的远比我曾经捐过的任何东西都值钱。尽管她很穷，但她给我的东西无价！

我看到了布基纳法索人民令人始料未及的美丽，深深地感受到穷苦人民内心的尊严。惭愧之余，我希望这枚硬币永远伴随着我。一枚小小的硬币，彻底改变了我的观念。

邪恶的僵尸伸手抢夺了三叶草的东西，甚至威胁到了它的安全，生气、愤怒、恼火一起涌上心头。战胜它、驱赶它、排斥它，对僵尸毫不留情。三叶草会怎样？正当主人公厌倦了布基纳法索的一切时，偶尔发现邪恶中也有正直，也有渴望和平友善的自尊。一枚小小的硬币，化解了主人公心中的怨。

三叶草篇
Forget and Forgive

It's okay, Mum!
没事的，妈妈！

As I sat perched (置于高处) in the second-floor window of our brick schoolhouse that afternoon, my heart began to sink further with each passing car. This was a day I'd looked forward to for weeks: Miss Pace's fourth-grade, end-of-the-year party.

I had happily volunteered my mother when Miss Pace requested cookie volunteers. Mom's chocolate chips reigned (统治) supreme on our block, and I knew they'd be a hit with my classmates. But two o'clock passed, and there was no sign of her. Most of the other mothers had already come and gone. My mother was missing in action.

"Don't worry, Robbie, she'll be along soon," Miss Pace said as I gazed forlornly (可怜地) down at the street. I looked at the wall clock just in time to see its black minute hand shift to half-past.

Around me, the noisy party raged on, but I wouldn't leave my window watch post. Miss Pace did her best to coax (哄骗) me away, but I just stayed there, holding out hope that the familiar family car would round the corner, carrying my rightfully embarrassed mother with a tin of her famous cookies tucked under her arm.

The three o'clock bell soon jolted (使震惊) me from my thoughts and I dejectedly (沮丧地) grabbed my book bag from my desk and shuffled (慢吞吞) out the door for home.

On the walk to home, I plotted (策划) my revenge. I would slam (砰地关上) the front door upon entering, refuse to return her hug when she rushed over to me, and vow never to speak to her again.

The house was empty when I arrived and I looked for a note on the refrigerator that might explain my mother's absence, but found none. My chin quivered with a mixture of heartbreak and rage. For the first time in my life, my mother had let me down.

I was lying face-down on my bed upstairs when I heard her come through the front door.

"Robbie," she called out a bit urgently. "Where are you?"

I could then hear her darting frantically (疯狂地) from room to room, wondering where I could be. I remained silent. In a moment, she mounted (爬上) the steps. When she entered my room and sat beside me on my bed, I didn't move but instead stared blankly into my pillow refusing to acknowledge her presence.

"I'm so sorry, honey," she said. "I just forgot. I got busy and forgot — plain and simple."

I still didn't move. "Don't forgive her," I told myself. "She humiliated (羞辱) you. She forgot you. Make her pay."

Then my mother did something completely unexpected. She began to laugh. I could feel her shudder as the laughter shook her. It began quietly at first and then increased violently.

I was incredulous (不相信的). How could she laugh at a time like this? I rolled over and faced her, ready to let her see the rage and disappointment in my eyes.

But my mother wasn't laughing at all. She was crying. "I'm so sorry," she sobbed. "I let you down. I let my little boy down."

She sank down on the bed and began to weep like a little girl. I was dumbstruck (目瞪口呆的). I had never seen my mother cry.

"It's okay, Mom." I stammered (结结巴巴地说) as I reached out and gently stroked her hair. "We didn't even need those cookies. There was plenty of stuff to eat. Don't cry. It's all right. Really."

My words, as inadequate as they sounded to me, prompted my mother to sit up. She wiped her eyes, and a slight smile began to crease her tear-stained cheeks. I smiled back awkwardly (笨拙的), and she pulled me to her.

We didn't say another word. We just held each other in a long, silent embrace. When we came to the point where I would usually pull away, I decided that, this time, I could hold on, perhaps, just a little bit longer. (603 words)

(Extracted from"http://www.chinadaily.com.cn/language_tips/book/2010-04/12/.htm")

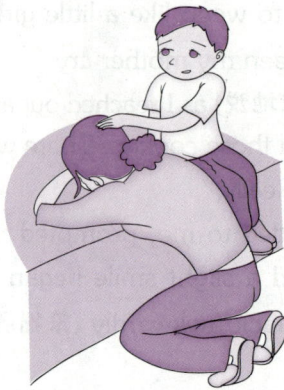

译
文

忘却与原谅

那天下午我坐在学校二楼的窗前,我的心随着来往的车辆一点点地下沉。这是我期盼了很久的一天:蓓丝小姐四年级毕业庆典。

当蓓丝小姐需要一个自愿提供自制饼干的人时我毛遂自荐我的妈妈。我妈妈的巧克力脆片是我最喜欢的,是整条街最好吃的。我相信它一定会在全班引起轰动。但是两点钟到了,始终没有妈妈的踪影。只见其他小朋友的妈妈进进出出。我的妈妈就要错过毕业庆典了。

"别担心,罗比,她很快会来的。"蓓丝小姐看到我可怜地往街道上张望时说。我看着墙上的钟,只见黑色的指针已经划过半个小时。

在我的周围是喧闹的庆典。但我不能离开我的瞭望窗口。蓓丝小姐用各种方式哄骗我去加入庆典。但是我仍旧一动也不动地待在那儿。满怀希望地想看到熟悉的小汽车驶过拐角,带来手拿饼干、兴奋而紧张的妈妈。

三点的钟声打破了我的思绪。我沮丧地收拾好书包,慢吞吞地出门往家走。

在回家的路上,我酝酿着我的复仇计划。我将要"砰"的关上前门,拒绝她的拥抱,发誓不再和她说话。

当我进门时,房子里空空的。我期望能在冰箱上看到妈妈的托辞留言条。但是,没有。我的下巴由于心碎和愤怒而不停地抖动。这是我人生中的第一次,妈妈让我失望了。

当我听到妈妈从前门进屋的声音时,我将头深深地埋向床里。

"罗比,"她焦急地喊,"你在哪儿呀?"

我能听得到她疯狂地一间屋子接着一间屋子地找我，猜想我在哪儿。我一直沉默着不出声。就在这时，妈妈爬上楼，进入我的房间，坐在我的身旁。我没动，只是死死地盯着枕头，不理她。

"对不起，亲爱的，"她说，"我忘了，我太忙了，真的忘了。"

我仍然没动。"不原谅她，"我对自己说，"她羞辱了你，忘了你，让她补偿。"

然后我感觉妈妈做了件不可思议的事。她开始笑了。我能感到她笑着抖动着肩膀。刚开始声音很小，然后慢慢变大变大。

我不能相信，这时她还能笑。我翻过身，看着她，想让她看到我眼里的愤怒和失望。

但是妈妈没有笑，她是在哭。"对不起，"她抽泣着说，"我让你失望了，我让我的儿子失望了。"

她倒向床，像一个小女孩一样的哭泣。我惊呆了。我从来没见过妈妈哭。

"没事的，妈妈。"我结结巴巴地说。我伸出手轻轻地抚摸着她的头发。"我不需要饼干，我们有很多其他东西可以吃。没事的。真的。"

那些安慰的话不由自主地从我的嘴里说出来，妈妈立即停止了哭泣，坐了起来。她擦了擦眼睛，一丝宽慰的笑掠过她满是泪痕的双颊。我笨拙地和她一起笑，由着她将我揽入怀中。

我们都不说话，只是持久地、默默地抱在一起。当这一刻到来时，我不想将其挥去。我决定就这样紧紧地、长久地抱着妈妈。

妈妈宽广的胸怀永远是我们最温暖的怀抱，即使我们做错了事，也永远对我们不离不弃。小男孩用和妈妈一样宽广的胸怀留住信任和关爱，用理智的选择来感化僵冷的心，用强大的内心来包容，用理智的选择来感化僵冷的心魔，换得了和妈妈间的和平。简简单单，做了你就会明白。

三叶草篇
Lifetime Catch

> You'll have to put it back, son.
> 你得把它放回去，孩子。

He was 11 years old and went fishing every chance he got from the dock at his family's cabin on an island in the middle of a New Hampshire lake.

On the day before the bass (鲈鱼) season opened, he and his father were fishing early in the evening, catching sunfish and perch with worms. Then he tied on a small silver lure (诱饵) and practiced casting. The lure struck the water and caused colored ripples in the sunset, and then silver ripples (波纹) as the moon rose over the lake.

When his pea pole doubled over, he knew something huge was on the other end. His father watched with admiration (赞赏) as the boy skillfully worked the fish alongside the dock.

Finally, he very gingerly (慎重地) lifted the exhausted fish from the water. It was the largest one he had ever seen, but it was a bass.

The boy and his father looked at the handsome fish, gills (鱼鳃) playing back and forth in the moonlight. The father lit a match and looked at his watch. It was 10 P.M. — two hours before the season opened. He looked at the fish, then at the boy.

"You'll have to put it back, son." he said.

"Dad!" cried the boy.

"There will be other fish," said his father.

"Not as big as this one," cried the boy.

He looked around the lake. No other fishermen or boats were anywhere around in the moonlight. He looked again at his father. Even though no one had seen them, nor could anyone ever know what time he caught the fish, the boy could tell by the clarity (清楚) of his father's voice that the decision was not negotiable (可协商的). He slowly worked the hook out of the lip of the huge bass and lowered it into the black water.

The creature swished its powerful body and disappeared. The boy suspected that he would never again see such a great fish.

That was 34 years ago. Today, the boy is a successful architect in New York City. His father's cabin is still there on the island in the middle of the lake. He takes his own son and daughters fishing from the same dock.

And he was right. He has never again caught such a magnificent fish as the one he landed that night long ago. But he does see that same fish — again and again — every time he comes up against a question of ethics (伦理，道德).

For, as his father taught him, ethics are simple matters of right and wrong. It is only the practice of ethics that is difficult. Do we do right when no one is looking? Do we refuse to cut corners to get the design in on time? Or refuse to trade stocks based on information that we know we aren't supposed to have?

We would if we were taught to put the fish back when we were young. For we would have learned the truth. The decision to do right lives fresh and fragrant (芳香的，愉快的) in our memory. It is a story we will proudly tell our friends and grandchildren. Not about how we had a chance to beat the system and took it, but about how we did the right thing and were forever strengthened. (533 words)

译文

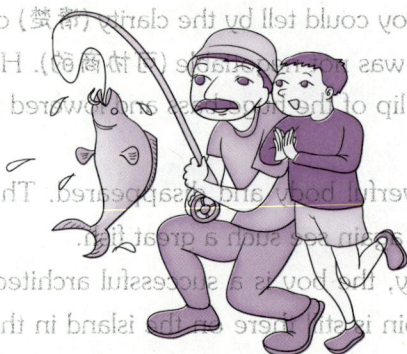

一生的收获

当他11岁时，只要一有机会，就会到他家在新汉普郡湖心岛上的小屋的那个码头钓鱼。

鲈鱼季节解禁开放的前一天晚上，他和父亲早早开始准备，用小虫作诱饵钓太阳鱼和鲈鱼。他系上鱼饵，练习如何抛线。鱼钩击在水面，在夕阳中漾起一片金色的涟漪，夜晚月亮升出湖面时，涟漪就成了银色。

当鱼竿向下弯的时候，他知道线的另一端一定上钩了一条大鱼。父亲看着他技巧娴熟地在码头边和鱼周旋，眼神充满赞赏。最后他小心翼翼地将筋疲力尽的鱼提出水面。这是他所见过的最大的一条鱼，但这是一条鲈鱼。男孩和他父亲看着这条漂亮的鱼，它的鱼鳃在月光下一张一翕。父亲点燃一根火柴，看了看表十点了，离开禁还有两个小时。他看了看鱼，又看了看男孩。

"孩子，你得把它放回去。"他说道。

"爸爸！"男孩叫道。

"不是还有其他的鱼嘛。"父亲说道。

"但没见过这么大的，"男孩叫道。

他环视了一遍湖心岛。月光下，没有其他的渔民或船只。在附近他又看了看他父亲。从父亲不可动摇的语气中，他知道这个决定没有商量的余地，即便没有人看到他们，也更无从得知他们何时钓到了鱼。他慢慢地将鱼钩从大鲈鱼的唇上取下，然后蹲下将鱼放回水中。

鱼儿摆动着它强健的身躯，消失在水中。男孩想，他可能再也看不到这么大的鱼了。

那是34年前的事了。现在，男孩是纽约的一个成功的建筑师。他父亲的小屋依然在湖心岛上，他仍然带着自己的儿女在同一个码头钓鱼。

他猜得没错。自那次以后，他再也没有见过那么大的鱼了。但每次当他面临道德难题而左右为难的时候，他的眼前总是浮现出那条鱼。

他父亲曾告诉他，道德就如同简单的对和错的判断题，但要付诸行动却很难。在没人瞧见的时候，我们是否能够坚持始终如一？为了将图纸及时送到，我们是不是也会抄近路？或者在明知道不可以的情况下，仍将公司股份卖掉？

在我们还小的时候，如果有人要求我们把鱼放回去，我们会这样做，因为我们学到了真理。正确的决定在我们的记忆里变得深刻而清晰。这个故事我可以骄傲地讲给朋友和子孙们听，不是关于如何攻击和战胜某种体制，而是如何做出正确的决定，从而变得无比坚强。

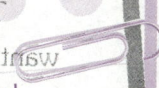

做决定很难，做正确的决定难上加难。当一道德难题摆在面前时，用何种方式战胜它，将是一个巨大的考验。正如人生会遇到很多决定，是要偏离正直的底线，取舍就在一念之间。放掉大鱼，再也钓不到如此大的鱼；留着大鱼，再也保持不了正直的本色。答案显而易见，三叶草会做到，那我们呢？

之
五

三叶草篇
Five Peas

I want to go to a place where I can bring happiness to others.

我想到能为别人带来欢乐的地方去。

There are five peas (豌豆) in a bean pod (豆荚). When they are mature, a small boy picks it and opens it.

The small boy puts the first one into an air gun.

"Ping"...the pea is shot out. It says happily, "I will fly to the sky!"

The small boy asks the second one, "Where do you want to go?"

The second pea says, "I want to fly to the Sun."

So, the second one is shot out, who says, "I will fly to the sun!"

The third one and the forth one are afraid to be put into the air gun. They scoot away.

The small boy gets out the fifth one and asks it, "Where do you want to go?"

The fifth one says, "I want to go to a place where I can bring happiness to others."

The small boy puts it into the air gun and says, "You are considerate!" He pulls the trigger and the pea flies into a flower pot. The flower pot's owner is poor. The mother has a sick daughter, who has been ill for years. The girl is very weak and looks miserable.

One day, Mum goes out to work. The little girl lies by the flowers pots on the balcony (阳台) in the sun. The bud (花蕾) stretches out its leaves, which seems to dance and it tells the little girl, "you will get better!"

When Mum comes back, the little girl says, "Mum, I found a little shoot." Mum says, "Oh, it is a little pea shoot. How do you feel today?" "I feel much better! In the sun, I feel warm and comfortable. I will soon be well." Mum says happily, "I hope my daughter will grow up as this little pea shoot!" So, mum puts a bamboo stick there and ties a string so that the shoot can grow along it.

From then on, the little girl lies beside the little pea plant, talks with it and sings songs for it. The pea plant grows day by day. Little by little the girl also recovers.

Finally, the pea plant blooms. It has a brilliant pink flower. The little girl kisses it. She smiles healthily and happily, her eyes shine; she thanks God for sending her the beautiful angel — the pea flower. Mum says, "Thank you, pea flower! You made my daughter happy and helped her fight the sickness and get well!"

Then, the little boy passes by the window. The pea flower waves its branches, and seems to say, "Look! I fulfilled (完成) my promise. I am such a happy flower!" (430 words)

(Extracted from "http://www.kekenet.com/read/201112/166218.shtml")

译文

五颗小豌豆

在一个豆荚里，长着五颗小豌豆。当它们成熟了的时候，一个小男孩捡到豆荚并剥开了它。

小男孩把第一颗豌豆放进一支气枪里。

"砰"的一声，豌豆射了出去。这颗豌豆欢呼着说："我要飞到天上去啦！"

小男孩问第二颗豌豆："你想到哪里去呀？"

豌豆说："我想到太阳上去。"

于是，第二颗豌豆被射了出去，它一边飞一边喊着："我要飞到太阳身边去了！"

第三颗、第四颗豌豆怕被装进气枪里，就悄悄地溜走了。

小男孩拿出第五颗豌豆，问："你想到哪里去呀？"

豌豆说："我想到能为别人带来欢乐的地方去。"

小男孩把豌豆装进气枪里说："你是最关心别人的！"小男孩一扣扳机，豌豆就飞到了一个窗台上的花盆里。花盆的主人家是一户穷人，妈妈带着一个生病的女儿。小姑娘已经病了一年多了，身体非常虚弱，看起来十分可怜。

这天，妈妈又出去干活了。小姑娘挨着花盆躺在阳台上晒太阳。忽然，她发现窗台上的花盆里长出了一颗小嫩芽。太阳照在小嫩芽上。微风吹过，小嫩芽舒展着自己的叶子，像是在跳舞，又像是在告诉小姑娘："你的病会好的！"

妈妈晚上回来的时候，小姑娘高兴地说："妈妈，今天我发现了一颗小嫩芽。它说我的病会好的。"妈妈说："噢，那是一颗豌豆苗，你今天感觉怎么样啊？"小姑娘说："我感到好多了！太阳照在我身上。"妈妈高兴地说："但愿如此啊！我的女儿会像这颗豌豆苗一样欢快地成长！"于是，妈妈用一根小竹竿把豌豆苗支撑起来，又从上面牵了一根线，好让豌豆苗盘绕着向上长。

从此，小姑娘每天都陪着豌豆苗，和它说话，为它唱歌。豌豆苗一天天长大了，小姑娘的病也一天天好了。

终于，豌豆苗开花了。粉红色的豌豆花鲜艳极了。小姑娘把脸贴近花瓣，轻轻地亲吻着。她的脸上露出健康幸福的微笑。她的眼睛闪闪发亮。她在心里感谢上帝派来的美丽天使——豌豆花。妈妈高兴地说："非常感谢你呀，豌豆花！你使我的女儿充满了欢乐，使她战胜了疾病，重新健康起来！"

这时，玩气枪的小男孩从窗下经过。豌豆花轻轻地摇了摇枝条，好像是在说："瞧，我实现了我自己的诺言。我是一朵快乐的花儿！"

这个故事让我们感到，和平、正直、奉献、快乐其实都很简单。三叶草是和平与正直的化身，它可以用自己并不强大的力量战胜僵尸，而非用武力，使得僵尸不得不悄悄退让。正如小豌豆，愿望很简单，将快乐带给别人。生活在现实中的我们，除了学习文化知识还有更值得学习的东西。和平与正直，神奇的三叶草，我们会努力！

无畏、直面挑战的大嘴花

大嘴花篇

Head up High

> Hold your head up high and face the world.
> 高高昂起你的头来面对世界。

I was fifteen months old, a happy carefree (无忧无虑的) kid until the day I fell. It was a bad fall. I landed on a glass rabbit which cut my eye badly enough to blind it. Trying to save the eye, the doctors stitched (缝纫) the eyeball together where it was cut, leaving a big ugly scar in the middle of my eye. The attempt failed, but my mama, in all of her wisdom, found a doctor who knew that if the eye were removed entirely, my face would grow up badly distorted, so my scarred, sightless (盲的，看不到的), cloudy and gray eye lived on with me. And as I grew, this sightless eye in so many ways controlled me.

I walked with my face looking at the floor so people would not see the ugly me. Sometimes people, even strangers, asked me embarrassing questions or made hurtful remarks (评论). When the kids played games, I was always the "monster". I grew up imagining that everyone looked at me with disdain (藐视), as if my appearance were my fault. I always felt like I was a freak.

Yet Mama would say to me, at every turn, "Hold your head up high and face the world." It became a litany (连祷) that I relied on. She had started when I was young. She would hold me in her arms and stroke my hair and say, "If you hold your head up high, it will be okay, and people will see your beautiful soul." She continued this message whenever I wanted to hide.

Those words have meant (意味着) different things to me over the years. As a little child, I thought Mama meant, "Be careful or you will fall down or bump into something because you are not looking." As an adolescent (青少年), even though I tended to look down to hide my shame (羞耻), I found that sometimes when I held my head up high and let people know me, they liked me. My mama's words helped me begin to realize that by letting people look at my face, I let them recognize the intelligence and beauty behind both eyes even if they couldn't see it on the surface.

In high school I was successful both academically (学术上) and socially. I was even elected class president, but on the inside I still felt like a freak (怪人). All I really wanted was to look like everyone else. When things got really bad, I would cry to my mama and she would look at me with loving eyes and say, "Hold your head up high and face the world. Let them see the beauty that is inside."

When I met the man who became my partner for life, we looked each other straight in the eye, and he told me I was beautiful inside and out. My mama's love and encouragement were the spark (鼓舞) that gave me the confidence to overcome my own doubt. I had faced adversity (逆境), encountered my problems head on, and learned not only to appreciate myself but to have deep compassion (同情) for others.

"Hold your head up high," has been heard many times in my home. Each of my children has felt its invitation (引诱). The gift my mama gave me lives on in another generation. (543 words)

(Extracted from "http://english.51ielts.com/a/info_bank/haowengongshang/2010/08.html")

译文

昂起你的头

在我十五个月大的时候，我也是一个无忧无虑的小孩，直到我跌倒那一天。那糟透了。我倒在一只玻璃兔子上，刚好割破了我的眼睛，那足以导致我失明。医生试图挽救我的眼睛，在我的眼球上将割破的地方缝到一起，在眼睛的中间留下了一道很大很丑的疤。这种尝试失败了，但是我的妈妈使尽浑身解数找到一位医生，从他那了解到如果将我的眼球彻底摘除，我的脸就会被彻底地毁掉。所以我的那个满是疤痕，盲的充满雾气灰暗的眼球一直伴随着我。当我长大了，这只看不到的眼睛在各方面限制着我。

我走路总是看地面，不敢抬起头，生怕被人嘲笑。有些时候人们，甚至一些陌生人，会问我一些尴尬的问题或做着伤人的评论。当和小伙伴们做游戏时我也总扮演"妖怪"。我渐渐地意识到每个人都用藐视的眼光看着我，似乎我的外表就是我的错误。我知道我是别人眼中的异类。

每当这种时候，妈妈总对我说："高高昂起你的头来面对世界"。这句话一度成为我的精神支柱。当我还小的时候她就这样告诉我。她揽我入怀，轻轻抚摸着我的头发，说道，"如果你高高昂起你的头，人们会看你美丽的灵魂。"无论什么时候当我想要躲避起来的时候，她总是这样对我说。

在我成长的过程中，这些话对我来说意味着很多不同的事情。当我是个小孩的时候，我想妈妈的意思是，"当心，你会摔倒的，你会撞上什么东西，因为你不看路。"当我是青少年时，我仍然试图低着头掩藏我的羞耻。但我发现有时候当我昂起头，让大家了解我时，他们是喜欢我的。妈妈的话帮助我意识到，让大家看到我的脸的同时，我要让他们了解我内在的美和智慧，这些从外表是不能被发现的。

上高中时，我在学业和社会活动中都很出色。我甚至被选为班长，但我仍然觉得自己是个异类。我最想要的是和大家一样。当我因此感到沮丧和难过时，我会和妈妈哭诉。她用慈爱的眼光看着我，对我说，"昂起你的头来面对世界，让他们看到你的内在美。"

当我遇到了我人生的另一半，我们相互对视时，他告诉我，我的内在和外在都很美。妈妈的爱和鼓励给了我自信，使得我克服了自己的困惑。我曾经身处逆境，面对挫折，但是我不仅仅学会了欣赏自己，同时懂得了如何鼓励别人。

"高高地昂起你的头"这句话在我的家里随时可以听到。当我的孩子遇到麻烦，我就会用这句话去鼓励他们。妈妈的话会铭记在世世代代家人的心里。

世界创造了一个独一无二的你，再也没有谁是跟你完全一样的。当大嘴花不得不面对很多无影僵尸的直视时，它会昂首挺胸，无畏地彰显自己的才华。当大嘴花用勇气和毅力回击了僵尸咄咄逼人的眼神时，它会发现很多人在为它喝彩欢呼，为它加油。"高高昂起你的头"，这不仅仅是妈妈对儿子的一种期盼，更是我们每个人面对生活，面对失意，面对挑战的一种态度。

之二

大嘴花篇
Wild Grass

> The grass is never pessimistic or sad, for it is tempered by resistance and pressure.
>
> 小草从不悲观和叹气，因为有了阻力和磨难才有历练。

There is a story which goes like this: someone asked, "What is the most powerful thing in the world?" There was a variety of answers. "Elephant." Someone said. "Lion." Another said. "Buddha's guardian (守护的) warrior." Still another said half-jokingly. As to how powerful the Buddha's guardian warrior was, no one was sure.

In fact none of the answers was correct. The most powerful thing in the world is the seed of plants. The force displayed by a seed is simply incomparable (无可匹敌的).

Here goes another story:

The bones of a human skull (头盖骨) are so tightly and firmly joined that no physiologist and anatomist (解剖学家) had succeeded in taking them apart whatever means they tried. Then someone invented a method. He put sonic seeds of a plant in the skull to be dissected (切开的) and provided the necessary temperature and moisture to make them germinate (发芽). Once the seeds germinated, they manifested (证明) a terrible force with which he succeeded in opening up the human skull that had failed to be opened even by mechanical means.

You may think this is too unusual a story to be grasped by the common mind. Well, have you ever seen how the bamboo shoots grow? Have you ever seen how frail young grasses grow out from under debris (残骸) and rubble (碎石)? In order to get the sunshine and bring its will to grow into play, no matter how heavy the rocks are and how narrow the space between the rocks is, it will wind its way up irresistibly (无法抵抗地), its roots drilling downward and its sprouts shooting upward. This is an irresistible force. Any rock lying in its way will be overturned. This again shows how powerful a seed can be.

Though the little grass has never been said to be herculean (力大无比的), the power it shows is matchless in the world. It is an invisible force of life. So long as there is life, the force will show itself. The rock above it is not heavy enough to prevent it from growing because it is a force that keeps growing over a period of time, because it is an elastic (有弹性的) force that can shrink and expand, because it is a tenacious (顽强的) force that will not stop growing until it is grown.

The seed does not choose to fall on fertile land but among debris. If it is filled with life, it is never pessimistic or sad, for it is tempered by resistance and pressure. The grass that fights its way out since the moment it is born can be called "strong" and "tenacious"; only the grass that fights its way up since its birth has the right to laugh with justified pride at the potted plants in glassed green houses. (443 words)

(Extracted from "http://www.putclub.com/html/ability/reading/prose/2011/0609/310.html")

‖ 无畏、直面挑战的大嘴花 ‖

译文

野草

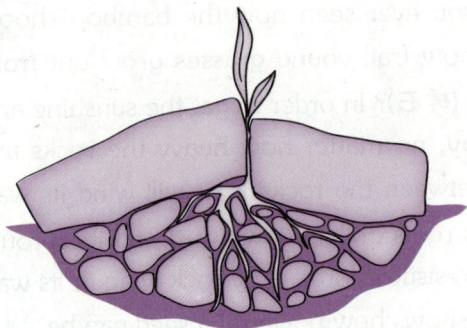

有这样一个故事。有人问：世界上什么东西的气力最大？回答各有不同，有的说"大象"，有的说"狮子"，有人开玩笑似的说是"金刚"。金刚有多少气力，当然没有人能知道。

事实上没有一个答案是完全正确的。世界上气力最大的，是植物的种子。一粒种子所显现出来的力量，简直可以超越一切。

这儿又是一个故事：

人的头盖骨，结合得非常密致与坚固，生理学家和解剖学家用尽了一切的方法，要把它完整地分割出来，都没有成功。后来有人发明了一个方法，就是把一些植物的种子放在要剖析的头盖骨里，给它以适当的温度与湿度，使它发芽。一发芽，这些种子便产生了可怕的力量，将一切机械力所不能分开的头盖骨完整地分开了。

也许你认为这个故事特殊得让常人不容易理解。那么，你看见过竹笋的成长吗？你看见过被压在瓦砾和石块下面的一颗小草的生长吗？它为着向往阳光，为着达成生的意志，不管上面的石块如何重，石块与石块之间如何狭窄，它必定要曲曲折折地，顽强不屈地透到地面上来。它的根往土壤里钻，它的芽往地面上挺，这是一种不可抵抗的力量，任何阻止它的石块，都会被它掀翻。这就是种子的力量。

没有一个人将小草称作大力士，但是它的力量之大，的确是世界上好多东西无法比拟的。这种力量是一般人看不见的生命的力量，只要生命存在，这种力量就要显现，上面的石块，丝毫不足以阻挡，因为它是一种长期抗战的力，有弹性、能屈能伸的力，有韧性、不达目的不止的力。

　　种子无论落在肥沃的土壤中还是落在凌乱的瓦砾中，它们都决不会悲观和叹气，因为有了阻力和磨难才有历练，它们仍旧有着顽强的生命力。因为小草生而顽强。只有小草才是如此的坚韧，也只有小草，才可以傲然地对那些玻璃棚中养育着的盆花哄笑。

　　　　面对僵尸时，大嘴花的力量非常渺小，小得让人感觉不到。但它从不屈服、不悲观也不叹气，直面凶险的敌人，即使会被吞噬，也迎面而上，毫不退缩。正像这坚韧的小草，简单不夸张，坚强有韧性。正所谓，"野火烧不尽，春风吹又生。"

之三

大嘴花篇
Follow Your Heart, Keep Your Dream

Follow your heart, no matter what.

心中有梦想，风雨不折腰。

I have a friend named Monty Roberts who owns a horse ranch (大牧场) in San Ysidro. He has let me use his house to put on fund-raising events to raise money for youth at risk programs.

The last time I was there he introduced me by saying, "I want to tell you why I let Jack use my house. It all goes back to a story about a young man who was the son of an itinerant (流动的) horse trainer who would go from stable (马厩) to stable, race track to race track, farm to farm and ranch to ranch, training horses. As a result, the boy's high school career was continually interrupted. When he was a senior, he was asked to write a paper about what he wanted to be and do when he grew up."

"That night he wrote a seven-page paper describing his goal of someday owning a horse ranch. He wrote about his dream in great details and he even drew a diagram (图解) of a 200-acre ranch, showing the location of all the buildings, the stables and the track. Then he drew a detailed floor plan for a 4,000-square-foot house that would sit on a 200-acre dream ranch."

"He put a great deal of his heart into the project and the next day he handed it in to his teacher. Two days later he received his paper back. On the front page was a large red F with a note that read, "See me after class."

"The boy with the dream went to see the teacher after class and asked, 'Why did I receive an F?'"

"The teacher said, 'This is an unrealistic (不切实际的) dream for a young boy like you. You have no money. You come from an itinerant family. You have no resources. Owning a horse ranch requires a lot of money. You have to buy the land. You have to pay for the original breeding stock and later you'll have to pay large stud (种马) fees. There's no way you could ever do it.' Then the teacher added, 'If you will rewrite this paper with a more realistic goal, I will reconsider your grade.'"

"The boy went home and thought about it long and hard. He asked his father what he should do. His father said, 'Look, son, you have to make up your own mind on this. However, I think it is a very important decision for you.'"

"Finally, after sitting with it for a week, the boy turned in the same paper, making no changes at all. He stated, 'You can keep the F and I'll keep my dream.'"

Monty then turned to the assembled (组合的) group and said, "I tell you this story because you are sitting in my 4,000-square-foot house in the middle of my 200-acre horse ranch. I still have that school paper framed over the fireplace." He added, "The best part of the story is that two summers ago that same schoolteacher brought 30 kids to camp out on my ranch for a week." When the teacher was leaving, he said, 'Look, Monty, I can tell you this now. When I was your teacher, I was something of a dream stealer. During those years I stole a lot of kids' dreams. Fortunately you had enough gumption (进

取心) not to give up on yours.'"

Don't let anyone steal your dreams. Follow your heart, no matter what. (560 words)

译文

追随心中
的梦想

我有个朋友叫蒙提·罗伯茨，他在圣思多罗有座牧马场。我常借用他宽敞的住宅举办募款活动，为了帮助青少年的计划筹备基金。

上次活动时，他致辞时说："我让杰克借用这里是有原因的。这故事跟一个小男孩有关，他的父亲是位马术师，他从小就必须跟着父亲四处奔波，男孩的求学过程并不顺利。高中时，有次老师叫全班同学写一份报告，题目是长大后的愿望。"

"那晚他认真地写了七张纸，描述他的伟大愿望，那就是想拥有一座属于自己的牧马场，并且仔细画了一张200亩农场的设计图，上面标有马厩、跑道等的位置，然后在这一大片农场中央，还要建造一栋占地4000平方英尺的巨宅。"

"他花了好大心血完成了报告，第二天交给了老师。两天后他拿回了报告，可是第一页上却打了一个又红又大的F，旁边还写了一行字：下课后来见我。"

"脑中充满幻想的他下课后带着报告去找老师：'为什么给我不及

格？'"

"老师回答道：'你年纪轻轻，不要老做白日梦。你没钱，没家庭背景，什么都没有。盖座牧马场是个花钱的大工程；你要花钱买地、花钱买纯种马匹、花钱照顾它们。你别太好高骛远了。'他接着又说：'如果你肯重写一个比较靠谱的愿望，我会重新给你打分。'"

"这男孩回家后反复思量了好几次，然后征询父亲的意见。父亲只是告诉他：'儿子，这是非常重要的决定，你必须自己拿定主意。'"

"再三考虑了好几天后，他决定原稿交回，一个字都不改。他告诉老师：'即使不及格，我也不愿放弃梦想。'"

罗伯茨此时向众人表示："我提起这故事，是因为各位现在就坐在200亩农场上占地4000平方英尺的豪华住宅内。那份高中时写的报告我至今还留着。他顿了一下又说："有意思的是，两年前的夏天，那位老师带了30个学生来我农场露营一星期。离开之前，他对我说：'罗伯茨，说来有些惭愧。你读高中时，我曾泼过你冷水。这些年来，我也对不少学生说过相同的话。幸亏你有这个毅力坚持自己的梦想。'"

不论做什么事，相信你自己，勿让别人的一句话击碎你的梦想。

大嘴花会张开大嘴吃掉僵尸。虽然得慢慢地咀嚼，但最终会胜利。有时候，我们执著地朝自己的目标前进，偶尔会停留在对过去的哀婉嗟叹中，去承担一些压力和不公平的言辞。但心中有梦想，风雨不折腰。真正有毅力的人，反而愈挫愈勇，更有韧性，就像罗伯茨一样坚定梦想，实现梦想。

之
四

大嘴花篇
A Coke and a Smile

> Okay, I'll try!
> 好吧，我试试！

I know now that the man who sat with me on the old wooden stairs that hot summer night over thirty-five years ago was not a tall man. But to a five-year-old, he was a giant (巨人). We sat side by side, watching the sun go down behind the old Texaco service station across the busy street. A street which I was never allowed to cross, unless accompanied (陪伴) by an adult, or at the very least, an elder sibling (兄弟姊妹). We sat watching the traffic. We counted cars and tried to guess the color of the next one to turn the corner.

"Thirsty?" Grampy asked, never removing the pipe (烟斗) from his mouth.

"Yes," was my reply.

"How would you like to run over to the gas station there and get yourself a bottle of Coke?"

I couldn't believe my ears. Had I heard right? Was he talking to me?

"Okay, I'll try." I replied shyly, already wondering how I would get across the street. Surely Grampy was going to come with me.

Grampy stretched his long leg out straight and reached his huge hand deep into the pocket. Opening his fist, he exposed a mound of silver coins. There must have been a million dollars there. He instructed (指示) me to pick out a dime (一枚硬币).

"Okay," he said, helping me down the stairs and to the curb, "I'm going to stay and I'll tell you when it's safe to cross. You go over to the Coke machine, get your Coke and come back out. Wait for me to tell you when it's safe to cross back."

My heart pounded. I clutched (紧握) my dime tightly in my sweaty palm. Excitement took my breath away.

Grampy held my hand tightly. Together we looked up the street and down, and back up again. He stepped off the curb and told me it was safe to cross. He let go of my hand and I ran. I ran faster than I had ever run before. The street seemed wide. I wondered if I would make it to the other side. Reaching the other side, I turned to find Grampy. There he was, standing exactly where I had left him, smiling proudly. I waved.

"Go on, hurry up." he yelled.

My heart pounded wildly as I walked inside the dark garage. I had been inside the garage before with my father. My surroundings were familiar. I heard the Coca–Cola machine motor humming even before I saw it. I walked directly to the big old red–and–white dispenser. I knew where to insert my dime. I had seen it done before and had fantasized (幻想) about this moment many times.

The big old monster greedily accepted my dime, and I heard the bottles shift. On tiptoes I reached up and opened the heavy door. There they were: one neat row of thick green bottles, necks staring directly at me, and ice cold from the refrigeration. I held the door open with my shoulder and grabbed one. With a quick yank, I pulled it free from its bondage (束缚). Another one immediately took its place. The bottle was cold in my sweaty hands. I would never forget the feeling of the cool glass on my skin. Coke in hand, I proudly marched back out into the early evening dusk. Grampy was waiting patiently. He smiled.

"Stop right there," he yelled. One or two cars sped by me, and once again, Grampy stepped off the curb. "Come on, now," he said, "run." I did. Cool brown foam (泡沫) sprayed my hands. I held the Coke bottle tightly; fearful he would make me pour it into a cup, ruining this dream come true. He didn't. One long swallow of the cold beverage cooled my sweating body. I don't think I ever felt so proud. (628words)

(Extracted from "http://edu.qq.com/a/20100122/000072.htm")

译文

可乐与微笑

我现在知道，35年前那个炎热夏夜和我坐在破旧的木楼梯上的老人并不高大，但对一个5岁的孩子来说，他却是一个巨人。我们并排坐着，看着太阳落在繁忙的街对面那个老德克萨克加油站的背后。除非有大人或至少一个哥哥或姐姐陪着，我从未被允许穿过那条街。我们坐在那儿观看繁忙的交通。我们数着过往的车辆，并猜想着下一辆拐过街角的汽车的颜色。

"渴吗？"祖父问我，嘴里还叼着他的烟斗。

"是的。"我回答说。

"跑到街对面的加油站去给你自己买瓶可乐怎么样？"

我简直不敢相信自己的耳朵，我没有听错吧？他是在跟我说话吗？

"好的，我试试。"我害羞地回答说，已经在想着该怎样穿过马路，祖父当然会跟我一起的。

祖父将他的长腿伸直，把他的大手伸进口袋。他张开手，露出了一堆宝贝似的银币。那里面一定有100万美元！他让我拿出一个1角的硬币。

"好吧，"他说着，接着他帮着我下楼梯到马路沿儿那儿去，"我站在这儿，什么时候穿过马路安全，我会告诉你的。你到对面的可乐机那儿买到你的可乐后再走回来。等着我告诉你什么时候过马路安全。"

我的心怦怦地跳着，紧紧地用汗手攥着那枚1角的硬币，兴奋得喘不上气来。

祖父紧紧地拉着我的手，我们一块儿看了看大街的前后左右。他走下马路沿儿，告诉我现在可以过去了。他放开我的手，我跑了起来。我从没有跑得这么快过。街道似乎很宽，我怀疑自己是否能跑到对面。跑到对面后，我回头寻找祖父，他正站在我离开他的地方，为我自豪地微笑着。我朝他挥了挥手。

"接着走，快点。"他喊道。

我的心怦怦乱跳着走进昏暗的修车站。我以前曾和父亲一块儿来过这里，对周围的一切都很熟悉。甚至在看见可口可乐机之前就听到了它的马达发出的嗡嗡声。我径直走向那台红白相间的巨大的老自动售货机。我知道该往哪儿插硬币，我曾看人做过并曾多次幻想有一天我也能亲身试一试。

那个老巨人贪婪地吞下我的硬币，我听见了瓶子移动的声音。我踮起脚尖伸手摸索着打开了它厚重的门。它们就在那儿！一排整齐的深绿色瓶子，瓶颈一个挨一个地凝视着我，冰箱里散发出冰冷的气息。我用肩膀顶着门，伸手抓住一个，迅速一拉，将它从捆绑中拉了出来，另一个立即占据了它的位置。瓶子在我汗津津的手中显得格外冰凉，我永远忘不了冰凉的瓶子接触我皮肤时的感觉。手拿可乐，我自豪地走回到外面，已是黄昏时分。祖父正耐心地等待着，并面带微笑。

"停在那儿，"一辆辆车在我面前飞驶而过，祖父再次走下马路沿儿，"现在过来，"他说，"跑过来！"我跑了起来，冰凉的棕色泡沫溅在我的手上。我紧紧地抱着可乐瓶，生怕他让我把可乐倒在杯子里，毁掉我的梦想，但他没有。我咕噜噜长长地吞下一口冰凉的可乐，冒汗的身体顿觉清爽无比。我认为自己再也没有过当时那样的自豪了。

故事中5岁的小男孩，怯生生地说"I'LL TRY."，内心是何等的挣扎，何等的恐惧。面对挑战，一步一步向前，在爷爷的帮助下，直击恐惧，买得可乐。正如年幼的大嘴花面对僵尸，不躲闪、不退让，受尽风雨洗礼，张开嘴巴，直面挑战。

大嘴花篇

The Smallest Fireman in the World

I just set my mind to something and I go out and do my best.

我下定决心做某件事情，就会全力以赴。

Training to be a fireman is a tall order for anyone, but the odds are bigger when you're 4 feet 2 inches tall.

Still, Vince Brasco, 19, hasn't let a little thing like height stops him from volunteering at his local fire department in Carbon, Pa., for the past four years, despite being born with achondroplasia (软骨发育不全), a type of dwarfism (侏儒症) that affects bone growth.

"I'll never let having achondroplasia stop me from doing anything," he told Barcroft Media. "I just set my mind to something and I go out and do my best. I wanted to be a fireman as a child so as soon as I was old enough to volunteer at 16, I did it."

Achondroplasia is a disability (残疾), but it hasn't affected Brasco's ability from going full blaze when it comes to fighting fires. Nope, he races to emergencies up to three times a day along with the rest of his crew, who all tower above him.

In fact, when there's a big fire, Brasco operates the hose at neighborhood blazes with his colleagues, helping to control the high-pressure jets.

A bum knee and various medical problems have required him to have 14 surgeries on his left leg. But that hasn't prevented him from doing the job.

Brasco says the doctor who gave him the physical exam to join the fire squad (班) tried to talk him out of it.

"It was a pretty heated argument because he doesn't know me," Brasco told PittsburghlLive.com. "He doesn't know what I can do. I'm just like everyone else. I just do things a little different. It's just different things I might need help with. I'm not afraid to ask for help."

Arnold (a spokesman for Little People of America) isn't shocked that the doctor who gave the physical had doubt, but he isn't surprised that Brasco has thrived either.

"For Vince and for other people with dwarfism, it's often social barriers against physical difference, not dwarfism, that stops them from doing things they want to do," Arnold said. "It is my hope that the example Vince sets will help others navigate the social barriers that stand in their way."

Although Brasco is only 87 pounds, he can bench-press 265 pounds. "I work out a lot — as much as I can down at my gym," Brasco said. "It really helps on the job. You need to be strong. Because I can lift so much, I'm handy (敏捷的) at salvage (抢救) jobs where we have to move heavy bits of metal debris — like after car accidents."

When there is a fire going, Brasco wears a custom-made fire suit while on the job.

When Brasco isn't fighting fires, he works part time at his local Best Buy and is studying to become a nurse to help others with health needs. But whenever he can, he responds to calls for the volunteer fire service.

"If I am in the area, then I just drop everything and run," he said.

His greatest challenge was when a neighbor's house caught fire last year.

"It was near my home and I knew the family inside. I was part of the crew outside and was firing water in through a second-floor window," he said. "It was the first time there was an accident involving someone I knew and I was really worried."

"Sadly, they lost their two German shepherds in the fire but all the people got out safe and I knew we did everything we could. I felt proud to be part of the crew that saved them." (584words)

(Extracted from "http://www.233.com/life/jili/20111223/123002137.htm")

世界上最矮的消防员

想成为一名消防员，对任何人来说都不是件容易的事请，尤其是当你的身高只有4英尺2英寸时。

然而，19岁的文思·布拉斯科却没让身高这样的小事，阻止他成为宾夕法尼亚州卡本市当地消防部门的一名志愿者。尽管出生时患有一种影响骨头生长的侏儒症——软骨发育不全症，但是现在他已经在消防部门里工作了四年。

"我决不会让软骨发育不全症阻止我做任何事情，"他告诉巴克罗夫特媒体。"我下定决心做某件事情，我就会全力以赴。我很小就想成为一名消防员，当我16岁，我就成为了消防志愿者。我实现了我的梦想。"

软骨发育不全症是一种残疾，但它并不影响布拉斯科灭火的能力。一点儿也不。他和同事们有时一天三次冲向紧急情况现场。当然了，他的所有同事都比他高一大截儿。

事实上，当有大火发生时，布拉斯科会和他的同事在火场外操作水枪，帮助控制高压水流的喷射。

疼痛的膝盖和各种健康问题，让他不得不在左腿上做了14次手术。但这并没有妨碍他的工作。

布拉斯科说，他加入消防队时，体检的医生劝说他不要当消防员。

"由于他不了解我，那次的争论相当激烈。"布拉斯科告诉PittsburghlLive.com。"他不清楚我能做什么。其实我和其他人一样，只是我所做的事和别人略有不同。在某些事上我可能需要别人的帮助。但我不怕寻求帮忙。"

体检的医生怀疑布拉斯科难以胜任消防员，当时阿诺德（美国侏儒组织的发言人）一点儿也不吃惊。现在布拉斯科成功了，他也不感到惊讶。

"对布拉斯科和其他侏儒症患者而言，往往是因为身体差异造成的社会障碍使他们放弃想做的事情，而不是侏儒症本身。"阿诺德说。"我希望布拉斯科会树立一个榜样，帮助他人跨越阻止他们前进的社会障碍。"

虽然布拉斯科只有87磅，但他在杠铃推举锻炼中能举起265磅的杠铃。"我经常锻炼——每次都在健身房躺下做推举锻炼。"布拉斯科说。"这对我的工作帮助很大。因为要做这项工作必须要强壮。因为我能举起很重的东西，所以我很擅长做需要移动重物的救援工作，比如移动很重的金属碎片——像交通事故后那样的。"

当有火灾发生时，布拉斯科会穿上特制的防火服去救火。

当布拉斯科不去救火时，他在当地的百思买做兼职并努力学习，想成为一名帮助他人恢复健康的护士。但如果消防服务需要他，只要他能去，他立刻就去。

"如果我在那个区域，我扔下东西就跑过去，"他说。

他经历的最大的挑战是在去年邻居房子着火时。

"起火的房子离我家很近，我认识里面的人。当时我在外面，通过二楼的窗户向里面射水，"他说，"那是第一次有我认识的人出现在事故中。我真的很担心。"

"遗憾的是，他们在火灾中失去了两只德国牧羊犬，还好没有人员伤亡。我知道我们尽了全力。能成为挽救他们生命中的一员，我很自豪。"

当命运冷眼旁观，给布拉斯科设计出种种磨难与考验；当恶魔嘲笑他身材矮小而无所作为，只有4英尺2英寸高的布拉斯科用毅力和无畏的坚持，给了它们狠狠的回击。犹如大嘴花咀嚼僵尸时，慢而危险，但始终坚持，直面挑战，毫不退缩。好样的布拉斯科，下定决心，勇往直前，命运奈我何！

有情、有义的寒冰菇

寒冰菇篇

A Boy and His Apple Tree

No matter what, parents will always be there and give everything they could to make you happy.

尽管如此，父母却总是有求必应，为了我们的幸福，无私地奉献自己的一切。

A long time ago, there was a huge apple tree. A little boy loved to come and play around it every day. He climbed to the tree top, ate the apples, took a nap under the shadow… He loved the tree and the tree loved to play with him.

Time went by…the little boy had grown up and he no longer played around the tree.

One day, the boy came back to the tree and looked sad. "Come and play with me," the tree asked the boy.

"I am no longer a kid, I don't play around trees anymore." the boy replied, "I want toys. I need money to buy them."

"Sorry, but I don't have money…but you can pick all my apples and sell them. So, you will have money." The boy was so excited. He picked all the apples on the tree and left happily. The boy didn't come back after he picked the apples. The tree was sad.

One day, the boy returned and the tree was so excited. "Come and play with me." The tree said. "I don't have time to play. I have to work for my family. We need a house for shelter. Can you help me?" "Sorry, but I don't have a house. But you can cut off my branches to build your house." So the boy cut all the branches of the tree and left happily.

The tree was glad to see him happy but the boy didn't appear since then. The tree was again lonely and sad.

One hot summer day, the boy returned and the tree was delighted. "Come and play with me!" the tree said.

"I am sad and getting old. I want to go sailing to relax myself. Can you give me a boat?" "Use my trunk to build the boat. You can sail and be happy." So the boy cut the tree trunk to make a boat. He went sailing and did not show up for a long time.

Finally, the boy returned after he left for so many years. "Sorry, my boy. But I don't have anything for you anymore. No more apples for you." the tree said. "I don't have teeth to bite." The boy replied. "No more trunk for you to climb on." "I am too old for that now." the boy said. "I really want to give you something…the only thing left is my dying roots." The tree said with tears. "I don't need much now, just a place to rest. I am tired after all these years." The boy replied. "Good! Old tree roots are the best place to lean on and rest. Come here, please sit down with me and have a rest." The boy sat down and the tree was glad and smiled with tears…

This is a story of everyone. The tree is our parents. When we were young, we loved to play with Mom and Dad… When we grow up, we leave them, and only come to them when we need something or when we are in trouble. No matter what, parents will always be there and give everything they could to make you happy. You may think that the boy is cruel to the tree but that's how all of us are treating our parents. (587 words)

(Extracted from "http://edu.chinawuliu.com.cn/yingyuxuexi/sysw/352895.shtml")

男孩和他的苹果树

很久以前有一棵高大的苹果树。一个小男孩每天都喜欢来到树旁玩耍。他爬到树顶，摘苹果吃，在树荫里打盹……他爱这棵树，树也爱和他一起玩儿。

随着时间的流逝，小男孩慢慢长大了。他不再到树旁玩耍了。

一天，男孩回到树旁，看起来很伤心。"和我一起玩吧！"树说。

"我不再是小孩了，我不能老是围着树玩了。"男孩答道，"我想要玩具，我需要钱来买。"

"很遗憾，我没有钱……但是你可以采摘我所有的苹果拿去卖。这样你就有钱了。"男孩很兴奋。他摘掉树上所有的苹果，高高兴兴地离开了。自从摘完苹果以后男孩没有回来。树很难过。

一天，男孩回来了，树非常兴奋。"和我一起玩吧。"树说。"我没有时间玩。我得为我的家庭工作。我们需要一个能遮风挡雨的房子，你能帮我吗？""很遗憾，我没有房子。但是，你可以砍下我的树枝来建房。"于是，男孩砍下所有的树枝，高高兴兴地离开了。

看到他高兴，树也很高兴。但是，自从那时起男孩没再出现，树有些孤独，伤心起来。

突然，在一个夏日，男孩回到树旁，树很高兴。"和我一起玩吧！"树说。

"我很难过，我在慢慢地变老。我想去航海放松自己。你能不能给我一条船？""用我的树干去造一条船，这样就能航海了，你就会高兴的。"于是，男孩砍倒树干去造船。他航海去了，很长一段时间未露面。

许多年后男孩终于回来了。"很遗憾，我的孩子，我再也没有任何东西可以给你了。没有苹果给你……"树说。"我没有牙齿啃。"男孩答道。"没有树干供你爬。""现在我老了，爬不上去了。"男孩说。"我真的想把一切都给你……我唯一剩下的东西是快要死去的树墩。"树含着眼泪说。"现在，我不需要什么东西，只需要一个地方来休息。经过了这些年我太累了。"男孩回答道。"太好了！老树墩就是倚着休息的最好地方。过来，坐在我身上，休息一会儿吧。"男孩坐下了，树很高兴，含泪而笑……

这是一个发生在我们每一个人身上的故事。那棵树就像我们的父母。我们还小的时候，喜欢和爸爸妈妈一起玩……当长大以后，便离开他们，只有在我们需要什么东西，或是遇到了困难的时候，才会回去找他们。尽管如此，父母却总是有求必应，为了我们的幸福，无私地奉献自己的一切。你也许觉得那个男孩很残忍，但我们又是如何对待我们父母的呢？

这棵苹果树就像我们的父母，永远呵护着我们，奉献着他们的一生。而我们作为孩子，仿佛僵尸一般，只有在我们需要父母，或是遇到了困难的时候，才会想到他们。我们是否应该反省一下自己？向有情有义的寒冰菇学习，也用我们的爱来回报父母对我们的养育之恩！

之二

寒冰菇篇
A Friend in Need

For many years thereafter, the two families watched the faithful friends frolicking and chasing each other down that well worn path between their houses.

自那以后多年中，两家邻居不时会看到这一对忠实的朋友嬉戏玩耍，在两幢住房间久踩成径的草地上相互追逐。

Brownie and Spotty were neighbor dogs who met every day to play together. Like pairs of dogs you can find in most any neighborhood, these two loved each other and played together so often that they had worn a path through the grass of the field between their respective (各自的) houses.

One evening, Brownie′s family noticed that Brownie hadn't returned home. They went looking for him with no success. Brownie didn't show up (露面) the next day, and, despite their efforts to find him, by the next week he was still missing.

Curiously, Spotty showed up at Brownie's house alone. Barking, whining (哀鸣) and generally pestering (纠缠) Brownie's human family. Busy with their own lives, they just ignored the nervous little neighbor dog.

Finally, one morning Spotty refused to take "no" for an answer. Ted, Brownie's owner, was steadily harassed (厌烦的) by the furious (狂怒的), adamant (坚定的、固执的) little dog. Spotty followed Ted about, barking insistently, then darting toward a nearby empty lot and back, as if to say, "Follow me! It's urgent!"

Eventually, Ted followed the frantic Spotty across the empty lot as Spotty paused to race back and bark encouragingly. The little dog led the man under a tree, past clumps of trees, to a desolate spot a half mile from the house. There Ted found his beloved Brownie alive, one of his hind legs crushed in a steel leg–hold trap. Horrified, Ted now wished he'd taken Spotty's earlier appeals seriously. Then Ted noticed something quite remarkable.

Spotty had done more than simply led Brownie's human owner to his trapped friend. In a circle around the injured dog, Ted found an array of dog food and table scraps which were later identified as the remains of every meal Spotty had been fed that week!

Spotty had been visiting Brownie regularly, in a single minded quest to keep his friend alive by sacrificing (献出) his own comfort. Spotty had evidently stayed with Brownie to protect him from predators (食肉动物), snuggling (偎依) with him at night to keep him warm and nuzzling (用鼻爱抚) him to keep his spirits up.

Brownie's leg was treated by a veterinarian (兽医) and he recovered. For many years thereafter, the two families watched the faithful friends frolicking (嬉戏) and chasing each other down that well worn path between their houses. (437 words)

译文

患难真情

布朗尼和斯波蒂是两只住着相邻的狗，每天它们都在一起玩耍。像那些几乎在任何社区能找到的成对的狗一样，它们俩互相爱慕，常在一起玩耍嬉戏，所以在各自房子与邻家相接的草地上已经踏出了一条小径。

一天傍晚，布朗尼的主人家发现它没有回家，搜寻一番也没找到。第二天，布朗尼依然没露面。尽管人们还在努力寻找着，到了第二周，它还是不见踪影。

奇怪的是，斯波蒂独自出现在布朗尼主人家，吠叫、哀嚎，还总是缠着布朗尼家里的人，但他们忙于自己的生活，没有在意邻居家这只神经质的小狗。

一天早上，斯波蒂终于拒绝接受"不"的回答。布朗尼的主人特德被这只暴怒的、不依不饶的小狗骚扰个不停。斯波蒂到处跟着特德，汪汪地叫个不停，然后窜到近处空地上，又窜回来，似乎在说："跟我来！情况紧急！"

最后，特德跟着发疯似的斯波蒂穿过空地，小狗停步奔回，用叫声催促着。它领着特德从一棵树下穿过，经过树丛，来到离房子半英里远的一处荒地。在那里，特德发现他心爱的布朗尼还活着，一条后腿被一个钢制捕捉器夹着。特德大为震惊，后悔当初没有认真对待斯波蒂的求助。随后，一幅非同寻常的景象映入眼帘。

斯波蒂不仅仅只是带领布朗尼的主人来到它被困的朋友跟前。在受伤的布朗尼四周，特德发现有一圈狗食和餐桌上的残羹剩饭——后来证实是在那个星期里每一餐斯波蒂都来给布朗尼喂吃的食物！

斯波蒂一直定时来看望布朗尼，一心一意要让它的朋友活下去，吃苦受累在所不惜。显然，斯波蒂一直陪着布朗尼，保护它免遭其他捕食动物的侵袭，夜间偎依着它为它驱寒，用鼻口拱它让它振作精神。

兽医治愈了布朗尼的伤腿。自那以后许多年，两家邻居不时会看到这一对忠实的朋友嬉戏玩耍，在两幢住房间久踩成径的草地上相互追逐。

所谓患难见真情！当自己的朋友遇到危难的时候，当他们被僵尸般侵蚀着的时候，你是否也应该向文中的斯波蒂小狗一样，真心帮助朋友，献出你的友情和爱心。所谓患难见真情。寒冰菇虽然外表冷酷，内心却充满了爱和情。

寒冰菇篇
Love Is Just a Thread

> But from this experience, I understand that love is just a thread in the quilt of our life. Love is inside, making life strong and warm.

但是从那一刻起，我明白了，爱情就像是生活中被子里的一根线。爱情就在里面，使生活变得坚固而温暖。

Sometimes I really doubt whether there is love between my parents. Every day they are very busy trying to earn money in order to pay the high tuition for my brother and me. They don't act in the romantic ways that I read in books or I see on TV. In their opinion, "I love you" is too luxurious for them to say. Sending flowers to each other on Valentine's Day is even more out of the question. Finally my father has a bad temper. When he's very tired from the hard work, it is easy for him to lose his temper.

One day, my mother was sewing a quilt. I silently sat down beside her and looked at her.

"Mom, I have a question to ask you," I said after a while.

"What?" she replied, still doing her work.

"Is there love between you and Dad?" I asked her in a very low voice.

My mother stopped her work and raised her head with surprise in her eyes. She didn't answer immediately. Then she bowed her head and continued to sew the quilt.

I was very worried because I thought I had hurt her. I was in a great embarrassment (尴尬；难堪) and I didn't know what I should do. But at last I heard my mother say the following words:

"Susan," she said thoughtfully, "Look at this thread. Sometimes it appears, but most of it disappears in the quilt. The thread really makes the quilt strong and durable. If life is a quilt (被子), then love should be a thread. It can hardly be seen anywhere or anytime, but it's really there. Love is inside."

I listened carefully but I couldn't understand her until the next spring. At that time, my father suddenly got sick seriously. My mother had to stay with him in the hospital for a month. When they returned from the hospital, they both looked very pale. It seemed both of them had had a serious illness.

After they were back, every day in the morning and dusk, my mother helped my father walk slowly on the country road. My father had never been so gentle. It seemed they were the most harmonious (和睦的) couple. Along the country road, there were many beautiful flowers, green grass and trees. The sun gently glistened through the leaves. All of these made up the most beautiful picture in the world.

The doctor had said my father would recover in two months. But after two months he still couldn't walk by himself. All of us were worried about him.

"Dad, how are you feeling now?" I asked him one day.

"Susan, don't worry about me." he said gently. "To tell you the truth, I just like walking with your mom. I like this kind of life." Reading his eyes, I know he loves my mother deeply.

Once I thought love meant flowers, gifts and sweet kisses.

But from this experience, I understand that love is just a thread in the quilt of our life. Love is inside, making life strong and warm. (509 words)

(Extracted from "http://edu.sina.com.cn/en/2005-03-27/32271.html")

译文

爱只是一根线

有时候，我真的怀疑父母之间是否有真爱。他们天天忙于赚钱，为支付我和弟弟的学费。他们从未像我在书中读到，或在电视中看到的那样互诉衷肠。他们认为"我爱你"太奢侈，很难说出口。更不用说在情人节送花这样的事了。而且，我父亲的脾气非常不好。经过一天的劳作之后，他经常会无故发脾气。

一天，母亲正在缝被子，我静静地坐在她旁边看着她。过了一会儿，我说："妈妈，我想问你一个问题。"

"什么问题？"她一边继续缝着，一边回答道。

我低声地问道："你和爸爸之间有没有爱情啊？"

母亲突然停下了手中的活，满眼诧异地抬起头。她没有立即回答。然后低下头，继续缝被子。

我担心伤害了她。我非常尴尬，不知道该怎么办。不过，后来我听见母亲说：

"苏珊，看看这根线。有时候，你能看得见，但是大多数都隐藏在被子里。这些线使被子坚固耐用。如果生活就像一床被子，那么爱就是其中的线。你不可能随时随地看到它，但是它却实实在在地存在着。爱就隐藏在里面。"

我仔细地听着，却无法明白她的话，直到来年的春天。那时候，我父亲得了重病。母亲陪他在医院里待了一个月。当他们从医院回来的时候，都显得非常苍白，就像他们都得了一场重病一样。

他们回来之后，每天的清晨或黄昏，母亲都会搀扶着父亲在乡村的小路上漫步。父亲从未如此温和过。他们就像是天作之合。在小路旁边，有许多美丽的野花、绿草和树木。阳光穿过树叶的缝隙，温柔地照射在地面上。这一切形成了一幅世间最美好的画面。

医生说父亲将在两个月后康复。但是两个月之后，他仍然无法独立行走。我们都很为他担心。

有一天，我问他："爸爸，你感觉怎么样？"

他温和地说："苏珊，不用为我担心。跟你说吧，我喜欢与你妈妈一块散步的感觉。我喜欢这种生活。"从他的眼神里，我看得出他对母亲深深的爱。

我曾经认为爱情就是鲜花、礼物和甜蜜的亲吻。但是从那一刻起，我明白了，爱情就像是生活中被子里的一根线。爱情就在里面，使生活变得坚固而温暖。

　　爱情的表现不仅仅是鲜花、礼物和甜蜜的亲吻。在平常生活中，爱情就像是生活中被子里的一根线，虽然不曾显露，但却使生活变得坚固而温暖。就好像寒冰菇一样，虽然外表给人以冰冷的感觉，但内心却是热情似火的。爱情的力量是巨大的，可以打败生活中的许多僵尸，使我们生活得更加美好。

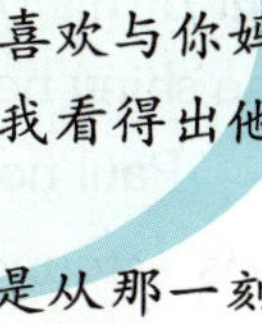

‖ 有情、有义的寒冰菇 ‖

寒冰菇篇

A Brother Like That

It is more blessed to give.
施比受更有福。

A friend of mine named Paul received an automobile from his brother as a Christmas present. On Christmas Eve when Paul came out of his office, a street urchin (淘气鬼，顽童) was walking around the shiny new car, admiring it. "Is this your car, Mister?" he asked.

Paul nodded. "My brother gave it to me for Christmas." The boy was astounded (使人大吃一惊). "You mean your brother gave it to you and it didn't cost you nothing? Boy, I wish…" He hesitated.

Of course Paul knew what he was going to wish for. He was going to wish he had a brother like that. But what the lad said jarred Paul all the way down to his heels.

"I wish," the boy went on, "That I could be a brother like that."

Paul looked at the boy in astonishment, then impulsively he added, "Would you like to take a ride in my car?"

"Oh yes, I'd love that."

After a short ride, the boy turned with his eyes aglow (炽热的，脸上发热的)，said, "Mister, would you mind driving in front of my house?"

Paul smiled a little. He thought he knew what the lad wanted. He wanted to show his neighbors that he could ride home in a big

148

automobile. But Paul was wrong again. "Will you stop where those two steps are?" the boy asked, He ran up the steps. Then in a little while Paul heard him coming back, but he was not coming fast. He was carrying his little crippled (跛足的) brother. He sat him down on the bottom step, then sort of squeezed up against him and pointed to the car. "There she is, Buddy (老兄，老弟), just like I told you upstairs. His brother gave it to him for Christmas and it didn't cost him a cent. And some day I'm gonna give you one just like it . . . then you can see for yourself all the pretty things in the Christmas windows that I've been trying to tell you about."

Paul got out and lifted the lad to the front seat of his car. The shining−eyed older brother climbed in beside him and the three of them began a memorable holiday ride.

That Christmas Eve, Paul learned what Jesus meant when he said: "It is more blessed to give." (376 words)

译文

兄弟情深

　　我有一个朋友叫保罗，他收到了一辆他哥哥送给他做圣诞礼物的新车。圣诞节当天，当保罗走出办公室时，看到一个男孩绕着那辆闪闪发亮的新车，十分赞叹地问："先生，这是你的车？"

　　保罗点点头："这是我哥哥送给我的圣诞节礼物。"男孩满脸惊讶，支支吾吾地说："你是说这是你哥送的礼物，没花你一分钱？天哪，我真希望也能……"

　　保罗当然知道男孩他真想希望什么。他希望能有一个像那样的哥哥。但是小男孩接下来说的话却完全出乎了保罗的意料。

　　"我希望自己能成为送车给弟弟的哥哥。"男孩继续说。

　　保罗惊愕地看着那男孩，脱口而出地说："你要不要坐我的车去兜风？"

　　"哦，当然好了，我太想坐了！"

　　车开了一小段路后，那孩子转过头来，眼睛闪闪发亮，对保罗说："先生，你能不能把车子开到我家门前？"

　　保罗微笑，他知道孩子想干什么。那男孩必定是要向邻居炫耀，让大家知道他坐了一部大轿车回家。但是这次保罗又猜错了。"你能不能把车子停在那两个台阶前？"男孩要求道。男孩跑上了阶梯，过了一会儿保罗听到他回来了，但动作似乎有些缓慢。原来他把他跛脚的弟弟带出来了，将他安置在第一个台阶上，紧紧地抱着他，指着那辆新车。只听那男孩告诉弟弟："你看，这就是我刚才在楼上对你说的那辆新车。这是保罗他哥哥送给他的哦！将来我也会送给你一辆像这样的车，到那时候你就能自己去看那些在圣诞节时挂窗口上的漂亮饰品了，就像我告诉过你的那样。"

保罗走下车子，把跛脚男孩抱到车子的前座。兴奋得满眼放光的哥哥也爬上车子，坐在弟弟的身旁。就这样他们三人开始了一次令人难忘的假日兜风。

那个圣诞夜，保罗才真正体会主耶稣所说的"施比受更有福"的道理。

　　"施比受更有福"。生活中人们不得不面对各种各样的困境，如同跟各种僵尸作斗争一样。当我们的朋友遇到困难的时候，我们不如学学有情有义的寒冰菇，将自己的东西和爱施予他人，也许在给他人带来意想不到的喜悦的同时，你也会感到无比的幸福。

之五

寒冰菇篇
Silent Love

> Such a gesture, I knew, was as far as Dad had ever been able to go in expressing his love.
> 我明白，这是他表达他对我的爱所能采取的方式。

After Mom died, I began visiting Dad every morning before I went to work. He was frail (虚弱的) and moved slowly, but he always had a glass of freshly squeezed (榨取的) orange juice on the kitchen table for me, along with an unsigned note reading, "Drink your juice." Such a gesture, I knew, was as far as Dad had ever been able to go in expressing his love. In fact, I remember, as a kid I had questioned Mom, "Why doesn't Dad love me?" Mom frowned. "Who said he doesn't love you?" "Well, he never tells me," I complained." He never tells me either," she said, smiling. "But look how hard he works to take care of us, and to pay for this house." Then Mom held me by the shoulders and asked, "Do you understand?"

I nodded slowly. I understood in my head, but not in my heart. I still wanted my father to tell me he loved me directly. Dad owned and operated a small scrap metal business, and after school I often hung around while he worked. I always hoped he'd ask me to help and then praise me for what I did.

"Why don't you hire someone to do that for you?" Mom asked Dad one night as she bent over him and rubbed his aching shoulders with a strong smelling liniment. "Why don't you hire a cook?" Dad asked, giving her one of his rare smiles. Mom straightened and put her hands on her hips." What's the matter, Ike! Don't you like my cooking?" "Sure I like your cooking. But if I could afford a helper, then you could afford a cook!" Dad laughed, and for the first time I realized that my father had a sense of humor.

Many years later, during my first daily visit, after drinking the juice my father had squeezed for me; I walked over, hugged him and said, "I love you, Dad." From then on I did this every morning. My father never told me how he felt about my hugs, and there was never any expression on his face when I gave them. Then one morning, pressed for time, I drank my juice and made for the door.

Dad stepped in front of me and asked, "Well?" "Well what?" I asked, knowing exactly what. "Well!" He repeated, crossing his arms and looking everywhere but at me. I hugged him extra hard. Now was the right time to say what I'd always wanted to. "I'm fifty years old, Dad, and you've never told me you love me." My father stepped away from me. He picked up the empty juice glass, washed it and put it away. "You've told other people you love me." I said, "But I've never heard it from you." Dad looked uncomfortable. I moved closer to him. "Dad, I want you to tell me you love me." Dad took a step back, his lips pressed together. He seemed about to speak, and then shook his head. "Tell me!" I shouted. "All right! I love you!" Dad finally blurted, his hands fluttering （颤动）like wounded birds. And in that instant something occurred that I had never seen happen in my life. His eyes glistened (湿物闪耀) , then overflowed. (535 words)

(Extracted from "http://hi.baidu.com/anna83wong/blog/item/a70f922cf5d7685a4ec226bf.html")

默默的父爱

在妈妈去世之后，我便在每天上班之前都去探望一下爸爸。他身体虚弱，行走缓慢，但是，每天他总是为我亲手榨好一杯新鲜橘子汁放在厨房桌子上，旁边有一张不签名的纸条，上边写着："把橘子汁喝了。"我明白，这是他表达对我的爱所采取的方式。事实上，至今我还记得，当我还是孩子时我问过我妈妈："为什么爸爸不爱我？"对此，妈妈皱起了眉头。"谁说他不爱你？""可是，他从来没告诉过我。"我抱怨道。"他从来也没告诉过我，"她说，脸上露出笑容，"不过，你看他拼命地干活为了养活我们，给我们买房子。"然后，妈妈抓着我的肩膀问道："你明白吗？"

我慢慢地点了点头。我脑子明白，可心里还是不明白。我仍然想要爸爸直白对我说他爱我。爸爸拥有并经营一家小的废金属处理厂。放学后，在他工作时，我经常在他身边玩耍。我总希望他会叫我帮忙，然后表扬我。

"你干吗不雇一个人来替你干那个活？"一天晚上妈妈为爸爸涂气味很浓的搽剂，俯身为他按摩酸痛的肩膀时问道。"你干吗不雇一名厨师？"爸爸反问道，并对妈妈难得地笑了一下。妈妈直起身子，双手叉在腰上："埃克，你怎么啦？难道你不喜欢我做的菜？""我当然喜欢你做的饭菜啦！可是，如果我雇得起帮手，那你就雇得起厨师啰！"我爸大笑起来，这是我生平第一次感到爸爸也有幽默感。

许多年之后，在我第一次看望爸爸的过程中，我喝完爸爸亲手为我榨的橘子汁之后，走过去搂住他，对他说："爸，我爱你。"从此我每天早上都这样做。可是，爸爸从未告诉过我，我拥抱他时他是什么感觉；而且我拥抱他时，他脸上从来没有任何表情。然后，一天早上，由于时间紧，我喝完橘子汁就向门口走去。

爸爸一步跨到我面前，问道："这个？""这个什么？"我问道，可我心中一清二楚。"这个！"他重复说，双臂交叉，东张西望，就是不看我。我格外使劲地搂了搂他。现在是说出我一直想要说的话的最佳时刻了。"爸，我已经50岁了，可你从来没有对我说过你爱我。"父亲转身走开了，他拿起那只空杯子，把它洗干净放好。"你告诉过别人你爱我，"我说，"可是我从未听你说过这话。"看上去，父亲感到非常不自在。我走近他，"爸，我想听你说你爱我。"他后退了一步，双唇紧闭。他好像要说话，然后又摇摇头。"告诉我！"我大声说。"行吧！我爱你！"父亲终于说出来了，他的手颤抖得像一只受伤的小鸟。在那一瞬间，出现了一生中我从未见过的情形：他的眼中噙着泪珠，最后终于潸然泪下。

在我们的记忆中，父亲总是很严肃、刚强的。父爱同母爱一样伟大，只是父亲表达爱的方式不同而已。恐惧时，父爱是一块踏脚的石；迷失时，父爱是一盏照明的灯；枯竭时，父爱是一湾生命之水；努力时，父爱是精神上的支柱；成功时，父爱又是鼓励与警钟。父爱是沉默的，犹如寒冰菇一样静静地守护着我们，在我们面对僵尸般的困境时永远默默支持着我们。

豁达、坚定的
猫尾草

之一

猫尾草篇
You Can't Afford to Doubt Yourself

No matter what happens, I'll always be there for you!

不管发生什么，我永远都会在你的身边！

On a spring evening some years ago, I decided to take in an off-Broadway musical where I heard Salome Bey sing for the first time. Even though half the seats were empty, Salome's voice filled the room and brought the theater to life. I was so moved by her performance that I decided to write an article to help promote her (though I'm not famous enough to do that).

The next day I phoned Salome Bey, acting like a professional (职业) writer.

"May I speak with Salome Bey, please?"

"Hello, this is Salome."

"Miss Bey, this is Nora Profit. I'm writing an article for Essence magazine (a well-known magazine), spotlighting (聚光) your singing achievements. "

Did I say that? Essence is going to have me arrested, I thought, (because it is not true.)

"Why, of course," said Salome. "Why don't you meet me at the studio?"

"Umm, all right," I said, trying to sound professional. "I'll see you next Tuesday."

Soon the interview time came. I, a bundle of nerves, took notes on a yellow pad, asking questions that all began with "Can you tell me...".

Back at home, I calmed down and began writing. But with every word I wrote, a small, stern (严厉的) voice inside me kept scolding (责怪): You lied! You're no writer! And , you've never even written a good grocery list.

I soon realized that fooling Salome Bey was one thing, but writing a story for Essence, a national magazine, was impossible.

Putting my heart into it, I struggled for days — rewriting and reediting my manuscript (手稿) countless times. Finally, I put my neatly typed, double-spaced manuscript into a large envelope, added my SASE (self-addressed stamped envelope), and dropped the package into a mailbox. As the mailman drove away, I wondered how long it would take before I'd get the Essence editor's "YUCK!" reply.

It didn't take long. Three weeks later there it was, my manuscript — returned in an envelope with my own handwriting. "What an insult!" I thought. How could I have ever thought that I could compete in a world of professional writers who make their living by writing? How stupid of me!

I threw the unopened envelope into the nearest closet and immediately forgot about it.

Five years later, while cleaning out my apartment, I came across an unopened envelope addressed to me in my own handwriting. Why would I send myself a package? I thought. (At that time I have totally forgot it.) To clear up the mystery, I quickly opened the envelope and read the editor's letter:

植物与僵尸

Dear Ms. Profit,

Your story on Salome Bey is fantastic. But please add some quotes (引言) and return the article immediately. We would like to publish your story in the next issue.

Shocked, it took me a long time to recover. Fear of rejection cost me dearly. I lost at least five hundred dollars and having my article appear in a major magazine — proof I could be a professional writer. More importantly, fear cost me years of enjoyable and productive writing.

I learned a very important lesson: You can't afford to doubt yourself. (537 words)

(Adapted from "Chicken Soup for the Soul")

你承担不起怀疑自己的后果

多年前一个春天的晚上，我决定去百老汇娱乐区外的一座剧院去听音乐剧，在那里我第一次听到萨洛米·贝的演唱。虽然剧院里有一半的座位空着，但是，萨洛米的歌声在整个房间里回荡，给剧院带来了生气。她的表演深深地打动了我，我决定写一篇文章来帮助提升她的人气（尽管我没有足够的名气那么做）。

第二天，我像一名专业作家一样，给萨洛米·贝打电话。"我可以跟萨洛米·贝通话吗？"

160

"你好，我就是萨洛米。"

"贝小姐，我是诺拉·卜罗费特。我正为《本质》杂志写一篇针对你演唱成就的报道（《本质》是著名杂志）。"

我真是那样说的吗？《本质》杂志会报警抓我的，我想（因为这根本就是我编的）。

"啊，当然，"萨洛米说，"那你到录音室来见我吧。"

"嗯，好的，"我说，努力使自己显得很专业，"下星期二见。"

很快，采访的时间到了。采访中，我紧张异常，尽量鼓起勇气问问题，同时在黄色的卡片上记着笔记，所有的问题都是以"您能告诉我……"开始。

回到家，我平静下来，开始写这篇报道。但是，每当我写下一个字时，我内心里一个细小、严厉的声音就不停地指责我：你撒谎！你不是作家！你甚至连像样的杂货清单都没有写过。

我很快意识到糊弄萨洛米·贝是一回事，但是要想为国家级的杂志《本质》写一篇报道是根本不可能的。

我全身心地投入写作，努力地写了很多天，写了又改，改了又写。最后，我把整整齐齐隔行打印出来的手稿装进一个大信封里，加上一个贴足邮资并写明我姓名和地址的回信信封，然后，我把这个大信封丢进了一个邮箱里。当邮差把邮车开走之后，我就开始猜测需要多长时间才能收到《本质》杂志的编辑写着"垃圾"字样的退稿回复。

没用多长的时间，就三个星期，我的原稿又寄回来了——就放在我自己写的信封里寄回来的。"多么大的侮辱啊！"我想。我怎么从来就没有想过我怎么能同一群以写作为生的专业作家竞争呢？我是多么愚蠢啊！

于是，连信封我都没打开，直接就把它扔进了最近的一个橱柜里，然后很快就忘记了这件事。

五年后，我在清理公寓时发现一封没有拆封的信，信封上的姓名和地址是我自己的笔迹。我为什么给自己寄一封信呢？我想。（当时我已经完全忘记了五年前写稿这件事。）为了揭开这个谜，我很快拆开了信封，读到了下面的内容：

亲爱的卜罗费特女士：

你关于萨洛米·贝的报道妙极了。但是请在文章里增添一些引述，并立即把文章寄回来。我们将在下一期杂志上把你的报道登出。

太震惊了！过了很长时间我才恢复过来。对被拒绝的恐惧使我付出了昂贵的代价。我失去了至少500美元的稿酬和让我的文章在一份重要的杂志上发表的机会——这可是我能够成为专业作家的有力证明呀！更重要的是，恐惧使我失去了多年本来能够快乐地写出很多作品的宝贵年华。

我得到了一个非常重要的教训：怀疑自己是要付出高昂的代价的！

对"被拒绝"的恐惧使作者付出了昂贵的代价，这种恐惧就像一具僵尸立在你的面前。你是否应该像猫尾草那样勇敢、坚强地同自我怀疑作战呢？拿出你的制胜法宝，击败僵尸，美丽的家园就是你的了！

猫尾草篇
The Miracle of a Brother's Song

> Never give up on the people you love.
> 永远不要放弃你爱的人。

Like any good mother, when Karen found out that another baby was on the way, she did what she could to help her 3-year-old son, Michael, prepare for a new sibling. They find out that the new baby is going to be a girl, and day after day, night after night, Michael sings to his sister in Mommy's tummy (肚子).

The pregnancy progresses normally for Karen, an active member of the Panther Creek United Methodist Church in Morristown, Tennessee. Then the labor pains come. Every five minutes, every minute. But complications arise during delivery. Hours of labor (分娩). Would a C-section (剖腹产) be required?

Finally, Michael's little sister is born. But she is in serious condition. With siren howling in the night, the ambulance rushes the infant to the neonatal intensive care unit (新生儿重症监护室) at St. Mary's Hospital, Knoxville, Tennessee. The days inch by. The little girl gets worse. The pediatric specialist (儿科专家) tells the parents, "There is very little hope. Be prepared for the worst."

Karen and her husband contact a local cemetery (墓园) about a burial plot (墓地，安葬地). They have fixed up a special room in their home for the new baby, but now they plan a funeral. Michael, keeps begging his parents to let him see his sister, "I want to sing to her." he says.

After two weeks in intensive care, it looks as if a funeral will come before the week is over. Michael keeps nagging about singing to his sister, but kids are never allowed in Intensive Care. But Karen makes up her mind. She will take Michael whether they like it or not. If he doesn't see his sister now, he may never see her alive.

She dresses him in an oversized scrub suit (消毒服) and marches him into ICU. He looks like a walking laundry basket, but the head nurse recognizes him as a child and bellows, "Get that kid out of here now! No children are allowed." The mother rises up strong in Karen, and the usually mild-mannered lady glares steel-eyed into the head nurse's face, her lips a firm line.

"He is not leaving until he sings to his sister!"

Karen tows (拉) Michael to his sister's bedside. He gazes at the tiny infant losing the battle to live. And he begins to sing. In the pure hearted voice of a 3-year-old, Michael sings:

"You are my sunshine, my only sunshine, you make me happy when skies are gray…"

Instantly the baby girl responds. The pulse rate becomes calm and steady.

Keep on singing, Michael.

"You never know, dear, how much I love you, Please don't take my sunshine away…"

The ragged, strained breathing becomes as smooth as a kitten's purr (猫发出的咕噜声).

Keep on singing, Michael.

"The other night, dear, as I lay sleeping, I dreamed I held you in my arms…"

Michael's little sister relaxes as rest, healing rest, seems to sweep over her.

Keep on singing, Michael.

Tears conquer the face of the bossy (专横的) head nurse. Karen glows.

"You are my sunshine, my only sunshine. Please don't take my sunshine away."

Funeral plans are scrapped (取消) . The next day, the very next day, the little girl is well enough to go home! Woman's Day magazine called it "the miracle of a brother's song". The medical staff just called it a miracle. Karen called it a miracle of God's love!

Never give up on the people you love. (557 words)

(Extracted from "http://www.ebigear.com/news-196-72524.html")

哥哥的歌声带来了奇迹

和其他称职的母亲一样，当凯伦发现自己再次怀孕之时，她尽她所能去帮助自己三岁的儿子迈克尔接受即将出生的孩子。后来大家得知新生儿是女孩，于是一天天，一夜夜，迈克尔不停地唱歌给还在妈妈肚子里的小妹妹听。

凯伦住在田纳西州莫里斯镇，是卫理公会的虔诚信徒。凯伦的怀孕过程很顺利，终于到了生产的那一天。先是每隔5分钟疼一次，然后每分钟都会疼。生产的时候出现了异常，持续了好几个钟头。需要剖腹产吗？

迈克尔的妹妹终于出生了，但她的情况很糟。救护车呼啸着连夜把她送到田纳西州诺克斯维尔圣玛丽医院的新生儿重症监护室。一天天过去了，妹妹的情况却更严重了。儿科专家通知父母，"没什么希望了，请做好最坏的打算。"

凯伦与丈夫联系了当地的墓园商讨安葬地的事宜。他们本来在家里给孩子准备了一间儿童房，而现在他们却得筹备一场葬礼。迈克尔一直不停的央求父母让他见见小妹妹，他说："我想唱歌给她听。"

在重症监护室住了两周之后，小妹妹似乎坚持不了多久了。迈克尔一直吵着要给妹妹唱歌，可重症监护室禁止儿童进入。但凯伦下定了决心，不管别人愿不愿意，她都要带迈克尔进去。如果现在不让他看，他可能再也见不到活着的妹妹了。

她给他穿上大号消毒服，快步带他走进重症监护室。他看起来像个会走的洗衣篮，但还是被护士长给看出来了，护士长大叫，"把那个小孩领出去！这儿不让小孩进！"在凯伦体内产生了一股强烈的母性，这位平日里温柔的女性眼睛冷冷地盯着护士长的脸，嘴角显出坚毅的线条。

"在唱歌给妹妹听之前，他是不会出去的！"

凯伦拉着迈克尔来到妹妹床前。他凝视着这个即将离开人世的小婴儿，开始唱歌。迈克尔用他三岁孩子稚嫩的童音，发自内心地歌唱：

"你是我的阳光，我唯一的阳光，你让阴郁的天空充满欢笑……"

妹妹马上有了反应，脉搏变得平缓稳定。

迈克尔接着唱。

"你从不知道，宝贝，我是多么爱你，请别带走我的阳光……"

妹妹急促而紧张的呼吸变得如同心满意足的小猫般顺畅。

迈克尔接着唱。

"那天晚上，宝贝，在梦乡，我梦到揽你入臂膀……"

迈克尔的小妹妹终于轻松起来，可以休息了，她似乎逐渐在休息中康复。

迈克尔接着唱。

专横的护士长脸上滑落点点泪珠。凯伦则兴奋得涨红了脸。

"你是我的阳光，我唯一的阳光。请不要，带走我的阳光。"

葬礼取消了。第二天，真的是第二天，妹妹就康复出院了！《健康之友》杂志称之为"哥哥歌声带来了奇迹"。医生们只把这称之为奇迹。凯伦则认为这是上帝之爱的奇迹！

所以，永远不要放弃你爱的人。

当死亡—这具令人最畏惧的僵尸，即将夺走你亲人生命的时候，你是否应该像倔强的猫尾草那样坚持，并坚强地同它作战呢？拿出你的制胜法宝，让我们的爱来击败僵尸，永远不要放弃你爱的人！

之三

猫尾草篇
The Missed Blessings

What may appear as bad fortune may in fact be the door that is just waiting to be opened.

其实，表面上看起来像是坏运气的东西或许正是等待开启的幸运之门。

A young man was getting ready to graduate from college. For many months he had admired a beautiful sports car in a dealer's showroom (陈列室), and knowing his father could well afford it, he told him that was all he wanted.

As Graduation Day approached, the young man awaited signs that his father had purchased (购买) the car. Finally, on the morning of his graduation, his father called him into his private study. His father told him how proud he was to have such a fine son, and told him how much he loved him. He handed his son a beautiful wrapped gift box. Curious, but somewhat disappointed, the young man opened the box and found a lovely, leather-bound (皮面装订本，精装本) Bible, with the young man's name embossed (雕刻) in gold. Angrily, he raised his voice to his father and said, "With all your money you give me a Bible?" He then stormed out of the house, leaving the Bible.

Many years passed and the young man was very successful in business. He had a beautiful home and a wonderful family, but realizing his father was very old, he thought perhaps he should go to see him. He had not seen him since that graduation day. Before he could make the arrangements, he received a telegram telling him his father had passed away, and willed all of his possessions to his son. He needed to come home immediately and take care of things.

When he arrived at his father's house, sudden sadness and regret filled his heart. He began to search through his father's important papers and saw the still new Bible, just as he had left it years ago. With tears, he opened the Bible and began to turn the pages. As he was reading, a car key dropped from the back of the Bible. It had a tag (标签) with the dealer's name, the same dealer who had the sports car he had desired. On the tag was the date of his graduation, and the words... "PAID IN FULL".

How many times do we miss blessings because they are not packaged as we expected? Do not spoil what you have by desiring what you have not; but remember that what you now have was once among the things you only hoped for.

Sometimes we don't realize the good fortune we have or we could have because we expect "the packaging" to be different. What may appear as bad fortune may in fact be the door that is just waiting to be opened. (418 words)

(Extracted from "http://emuch.net/html/201201/4034126.html")

译文

错过的祝福

从前，有位年轻人即将大学毕业。数月来，他一直渴望得到某汽车商产品陈列室中的一辆跑车。他知道，他那富有的父亲肯定买得起这辆车，于是，他便跟父亲说他很想得到那辆漂亮的跑车。

在毕业典礼即将来临的日子里，年轻人等待着父亲买下跑车的消息。终于，在毕业典礼那天上午，父亲将他叫到自己的书房，并告诉他，有他这么出色的儿子自己感到非常自豪而且非常爱他这个儿子。接着，父亲递给儿子一个包装精美的礼品盒。年轻人感到好奇，但带着些许失望地打开礼品盒，却发现里面是一本精美的精装本《圣经》，上面以金子凸印着年轻人的名字。看罢，年轻人怒气冲冲地向父亲大喊道："你有那么多钱，却只给我一本《圣经》？"说完，便丢下《圣经》，愤怒地冲出房子。

多年以后，年轻人已事业有成。他拥有一所漂亮的房子，一个温馨的家庭。但当得知父亲年事已高，他想，或许应该去看看他。自从毕业那天起他就一直不见父亲。就在起程时，他收到一封电报——父亲已逝世，并已立下遗嘱将其所有财产转给儿子。他要立即回父亲家处理后事。

在父亲的房子里，他突然内心感到一阵悲伤与懊悔。他开始仔细搜寻父亲的重要文件，突然发现了那本《圣经》——还跟几年前一样新。他噙着泪水打开《圣经》并一页一页地翻着。忽然，从书的背面掉出一把钥匙。钥匙上挂着一个标签，上面写着一个汽车经销商的名字——正是他曾渴望得到的那辆跑车的经销商。标签上还有他的毕业日期及"款已付清"的字样。

我们多少次地与祝福擦肩而过，仅仅因为他们没有按我们想象中的样子包装好？不要在渴望得到没有的东西时损坏已经拥有的东西，但要记住一点：你现在所拥有的恰恰正是你曾经一心渴望得到的。

有时，我们并没有意识到我们已经拥有或本该拥有的好运，仅仅因为它的外表与我们想象中的有所不同。其实，表面上看起来像是坏运气的东西或许正是等待开启的幸运之门。

我们有时并未意识到自己已经拥有或本该拥有的好运，仅仅因为它的外表与想象中的有所不同。所以此时我们是否应该像猫尾草一样更加豁达一些，让这些表面上看起来像是坏运气的僵尸离我们远去，满足现在所拥有的这些，或许正是等待开启的幸运之门。

之四

猫尾草篇

The Story of Steve Jobs

> So you have to trust that the dots will somehow connect in your future.
>
> 因此，你们必须要相信，现在所学的东西总是能与未来联系起来的。

This is the text of the Commencement Address by Steve Jobs, CEO of Apple Computer and of Pixar Animation Studios, delivered on June 12, 2005.

And 17 years later I did go to college. But I naively chose a college that was almost as expensive as Stanford, and all of my working-class parents' savings were being spent on my college tuition. After six months, I couldn't see the value in it. I had no idea what I wanted to do with my life and no idea how college was going to help me figure it out. And here I was spending all of the money my parents had saved their entire life. So I decided to drop out and trusted that it would all work out OK. It was pretty scary at the time, but looking back it was one of the best decisions I ever made. The minute I dropped out I could stop taking the required classes that didn't interest me, and begin dropping in on the ones that looked interesting.

It wasn't all romantic. I didn't have a dorm room, so I slept on the floor in friends' rooms, I returned coke bottles for the 5¢ deposits to buy food with, and I would walk the 7 miles across town every Sunday night to get one good meal a week at the Hare Krishna temple. I loved it. And much of what I stumbled into by following my curiosity and intuition turned out to be priceless later on. Let me give you one example:

Reed College at that time offered perhaps the best calligraphy (书法) instruction in the country. Throughout the campus every poster, every label on every drawer, was beautifully hand calligraphed. Because I had dropped out and didn't have to take the normal classes, I decided to take a calligraphy class to learn how to do this. I learned about serif and san serif typefaces (灯芯体和衬线体), about varying the amount of space between different letter combinations, about what makes great typography great. It was beautiful, historical, artistically subtle (微妙) in a way that science can't capture, and I found it fascinating.

None of this had even a hope of any practical application in my life. But ten years later, when we were designing the first Macintosh computer, it all came back to me. And we designed it all into the Mac. It was the first computer with beautiful typography (排版，排印). If I had never dropped in on that single course in college, the Mac. would have never had multiple typefaces or proportionally spaced fonts (字体). And since Windows just copied the Mac. its likely that no personal computer would have them. If I had never dropped out, I would have never dropped in on this calligraphy class, and personal computers might not have the wonderful typography that they do. Of course it was impossible to connect the dots looking forward when I was in college. But it was very, very clear looking backwards ten years later.

Again, you can't connect the dots looking forward; you can only connect them looking backwards. So you have to trust that the dots will somehow connect in your future. You have to trust in something – your gut (直觉，本能)，destiny (命运)，life, karma (因果报应)，whatever. This approach has never let me down, and it has made all the difference in my life. (555 words)

译文

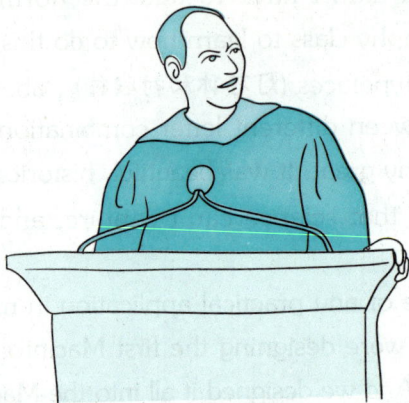

史蒂夫·乔布斯的人生故事

这是苹果电脑公司兼皮克斯动画公司的CEO史蒂夫·乔布斯于2005年6月12日在斯坦福大学毕业典礼上做的极富启发意义的演讲。

十七年过去了，我真的上了大学。但我却很天真地挑了一个和斯坦福大学一样学费昂贵的学校，光是学费就花掉了我父母辛辛苦苦积攒多年的积蓄，他们只是工薪阶层。在学校待了六个月后，我看不出这学费花得值得。我不知道我的人生计划是什么，也不知道大学能够如何帮助我找到这一目标。而且，我在学校念书会花掉父母一生的积蓄。于是，我决定辍学，并坚信这是一个正确的决定。在当时，这是一个相当骇人的举动，但今天回头看看，那是我做出的最明智的决定之一。辍学之后，我马上逃离了那些我对之毫无兴趣的必修课程，转而开始旁听那些看起来很有趣的科目。

但事情也并非全是美好的。辍学后我就没有寝室了，因此，我睡在朋友房间的地板上。为了有钱吃饭，我把可乐瓶子退回商店，只为了那5美分的押金，每周星期天晚上，为了吃一顿大餐，我还要走7英里的路，到城镇另一头儿的印度哈而克利须那寺。但我热爱这种生活。而且，许多我出于好奇和直觉而偶然去做的事，后来也被证明是非常值得的。我来为你们举一个例子。

当时，里德学院提供的恐怕是全国最棒的书法教育。走在校园里，每一幅贴在墙上的海报，每一张抽屉上的标签，都是漂漂亮亮的手写体。由于我辍了学，不用再去上常规课程，我便决定报名参加书法班，学写一手漂亮的字。在班里，我学到了灯芯体和衬线体，在不同字母组合间的间隙的变化，以及如何才能让印刷字体美观。那种美妙、古朴、艺术、微妙，是科学所不能达到的。我对之着了迷。

在当时看来，这些事物仿佛于我的人生没有任何实际的应用价值。但十年之后，我在设计第一台苹果电脑时，它们都重新浮现在我的脑海里，我们在设计电脑时好好地运用了它们，使我们的苹果电脑成为了第一台精致排版的电脑。如果我当时没有去旁听书法班，苹果电脑就不会有多字体选择，字母间也不会有匀称的间隙。而且，由于Windows系统是借鉴了Mac.系统的产物，如今所有的个人电脑都没有多字体选择和美妙的字母间隙，这也是有可能的。要是我从未辍学，我就不可能参加书法班，个人电脑也就不可能有这么精妙的字体排版，这些事情就像一个一个的点。当我还在学校时，是不可能看得出这些未来的来龙去脉的。但十年之后，再回头来看，一切就很明显了。

你们也是一样，现在要将未来看透是不可能的，只有在将来，事物间的联系才会显现出来。因此，你们必须要相信，现在所学的东西总是能与未来联系起来的。而且，你们还得坚信一种东西，不管是直觉也好，命运也罢，甚至人生，或是因果报应，无论什么都好。我的这种信仰从来没有让我失望，正是它使我的人生如此的与众不同。

这位世界上最有影响力的苹果公司的总裁—乔布斯在一生中始终坚持着自己的信仰，一步步地指引他走向成功。在人生中，那些你被迫做的一些事情以及不感兴趣的事情就如同令人畏惧的僵尸一般，剥夺了你人生的乐趣，甚至阻碍你成功的道路。你是否应该像坚韧的猫尾草那样坚持，始终坚信自己的决定，做自己真正感兴趣的事情。要始终坚持一种信仰，无论它是什么，它必定会带给你人生的转折和希望。

猫尾草篇
Father Can See My Success

"Dad came to all my games, but today was the first time he could see me play, and I wanted to show him I could do it!"

"父亲在天上，他第一次能真正地看见我比赛了！所以我想让他知道，我能行！"

A teenage boy lived alone with his father. The two of them had a very special relationship.

Even though the son was always "warming the bench", his father was always in the stands cheering. He never missed a football game.

This young man was still the smallest of the class when he entered high school. But his father continued to encourage him also made it very clear that he did not have to play football if he didn't want to. But the young man loved football and decided to hang in there.

The son was determined to try his best at every practice, and perhaps he'd get to play when he became a senior.

All through high school he never missed a practice but still remained a bench warmer all four years. His faithful father was always in the stands, always with words of encouragement for him.

When the young man went to college, he decided to try out for the football team as a "walk-on". Everyone was sure he could never make the cut, but he did. The coach admitted that he kept him on the roster (候选名单) because he always puts his heart and soul to every practice and, at the same time, provided the other members with the spirit and hustle they badly needed.

The news that he had survived the cut thrilled him so much that he rushed to the nearest phone and called his father. His father shared his excitement and was sent season tickets for all the college games.

This persistent young athlete never missed practice during his four years at college, but he never got to play in the game. It was the end of his senior football season, and as he trotted onto the practice field shortly before the big play-off game, the coach met him with a telegram.

The young man read the telegram and he became deathly silent. Swallowing hard, he mumbled to the coach, "My father died this morning. Is it all right if I miss practice today?" The coach put his arm gently around his shoulder and said, "Take the rest of the week off, son. And don't even plan to come back to the game on Saturday."

Saturday arrived, and the game was not going well. In the third quarter, when the team was ten points behind, a silent young man quietly slipped into the empty locker room and put on his football gear. As he ran onto the sidelines, the coach and his players were astounded to see their faithful teammate back so soon.

"Coach, please let me play. I've just got to play today," said the young man. The coach pretended not to hear him. There was no way he wanted his worst player in this close playoff (最后决赛) game. But the young man persisted, and finally feeling sorry for the kid, the coach gave in.

"All right," he said, "you can go in." Before long, the coach, the players and everyone in the stands could not believe their eyes. This little unknown, who had never played before was doing everything right.

The opposing team could not stop him. He ran, he passed,

blocked and tackled like a star. His team began to triumph. The score was soon tied.

In the closing seconds of the game, this kid intercepted a pass and ran all the way for the winning touchdown (触地得分)!

The fans broke loose. His teammates hoisted him onto their shoulders. Such cheering you've never heard.

Finally, after the stands had emptied and the team had showered and left the locker room, the coach noticed that the young man was sitting quietly in the corner all alone. The coach came to him and said, "Kid, I can't believe it. You were fantastic! Tell me what got into you? How did you do it?"

He looked at the coach, with tears in his eyes, and said, "Well, you knew my dad died, but did you know that my dad was blind?"

The young man swallowed hard and forced a smile, "Dad came to all my games, but today was the first time he could see me play, and I wanted to show him I could do it!" (699 words)

译文

父亲一定能看到我赢了

有一个男孩，他与父亲相依为命，父子感情特别深。

男孩虽然在球场上常常是板凳队员，但他的父亲仍然场场不落地前来观看，并且每次都在看台上为儿子鼓劲。

在进入中学的时候，男孩是班级中个头最小的，但父亲仍然继续鼓励他，并且也清楚地告诉他不用非得做一名橄榄球运动员。但是男孩热爱橄榄球，并且决定要坚持自己的梦想。

男孩在每次训练中力求做到最好，这样才能在四年级的时候有机会上场比赛。

整个中学时期，男孩没有误过一场训练，但在四年的中学里他仍然是一个板凳队员，而他的父亲也一直在看台上鼓励着他。

当男孩进了大学，他参加了学校橄榄球队的选拔赛。能进入球队，哪怕是跑龙套他也愿意。人们都以为他不行，可这次他成功了——教练挑选他进了候选名单是因为他永远都那么用心地训练，同时还不断给别的同伴打气。

入选橄榄球队的消息使男孩兴奋异常，他冲到最近的电话亭打电话给父亲。父亲和儿子一起分享喜悦并且收到了儿子寄来的所有大学比赛的赛季票。

这个有毅力的男孩在四年的大学里还是从未缺席任何一场训练，但还是从未得到过一次上场机会。转眼就快毕业了，这是男孩在学校球队的最后一个赛季了，一场大赛即将来临。在决赛前的一天，男孩小跑着来到训练场。一会儿，教练过来给他一封电报。

男孩看完电报，突然变得死一般沉默。他拼命忍住哭泣，对教练说："我父亲今天早上去世了，我今天可以不参加训练吗？"教练温和地搂住男孩的肩膀，说："这一周你都可以不来，孩子，星期六的比赛也可以不来。"

星期六到了，那场球赛打得十分艰难。当比赛进行到3/4的时候，男孩所在的队已经输了10分。就在这时，一个沉默的年轻人悄悄地跑进空无一人的更衣间，换上了他的球衣。当他跑上球场边线，教练和场外的队员们都惊异地看着这个满脸自信的队友。

"教练，请允许我上场，就今天。"男孩央求道。教练假装没有听见。今天的比赛太重要了，差不多可以决定本赛季的胜负，他当然没有理由让最差的队员上场。但是男孩不停地央求，教练终于让步了。

"好吧，"教练说，"你上去吧。"很快，在看台上的所有人，包括教练和队友都无法相信自己的眼睛。这个身材瘦小、籍籍无名、从未上过场的球员，在球场上无所不能。

对方没人能阻止他，他在场上奔跑、过人、拦住对方带球的队员，简直就像球星一样。他所在的球队开始转败为胜，很快比分打成了平局。

就在比赛结束前的几秒钟，男孩一路狂奔冲向底线，触地得分！赢了！

男孩的队友们高高地把他抛起来，看台上球迷的欢呼声如山洪暴发！

当看台上的人们渐渐走空，队员们沐浴过后一一离开了更衣间，教练注意到，男孩安静地独自一人坐在球场的一角。教练走近他，说："孩子，我简直不能相信，你简直是个奇迹！告诉我你是怎么做到的？"

男孩看着教练，泪水盈满了他的眼睛。他说："你知道我父亲去世了，但是你知道吗？我父亲根本就看不见！"

男孩哽咽着，勉强挤出一丝微笑："父亲来看过我以前所有的比赛，但今天他第一次能真正地看见我比赛了！所以我想让他知道，我能行！"

　　坚持并用心的训练，加上父亲不断的鼓励使一个男孩成为大学里橄榄球队的一名队员。尽管在这条路上充满着艰难，像无数邪恶的僵尸般阻拦着他前进的道路，但是他始终没有放弃，如同坚韧的猫尾草那样坚持，为了胜利的那一天，为了不辜负父亲的爱与期望，创造着奇迹！

宽容、友善的魅惑菇

魅惑菇篇
Tolerance Is a Virtue

You must know that tolerance is not cowardice, but a virtue.

你必须知道宽容不是软弱而是一种美德。

On August 23, 2004, the Athens Olympic horizontal bar final was going on vehemently (激烈地). Russian Nemov, 28, entered the arena third. He won the audience with the very difficult movement of rising high in the air and grabbing the bar, but when landing, he made a flaw — moving a step forward, so the referee only scored him 9.725 points.

At this moment, in the history of the Olympic Games, a rare instance appeared: the whole audience kept shouting "Nemov," "Nemov," and all rose, brandishing (挥舞) their arms and shooting their outrage to the referee long and loud. The competition was suspended. The fourth player, American Paul Ham, though ready, could only stand on the spot in embarrassment.

Faced with such a scenario (局面), Nemov who had withdrawn stood up from his seat, waved and greeted to the audience hailing him, bowed deeply and thanked them for their love and support. Nemov's magnanimity (宽宏大量) further kindled the audience's dissatisfaction. More boos rang while some of the audience even threw out their fists with thumbs down making indecent moves.

Against this enormous pressure, a referee was forced to score Nemov 9.762 points. However, such a score not only could not appease (安抚) the audience's discontent, but boos sounded again.

Upon this, Nemov displayed his charisma (超凡魅力) and magnanimity. He returned to the game and raised his right arm to pay tribute to the audience and deeply bowed to express his gratitude. After that, he extended his right index finger to make a gesture for silence, and then pressed his hands down to request and soothe the audience to remain calm and give Paul Ham a quiet condition.

Nemov's tolerance set the interrupted game for over minutes going on.

In that game Nemov didn't get a gold medal, but he was still a "champion" in the eyes of the audience; he didn't defeat the opponents, but he won the audience with his own tolerance.

When someone disagrees with you or offends you, don't lose your temper. Why? Because it is of no use to do so. You ought to be tolerant and keep calm lest you should quarrel with him. You must know that tolerance is not cowardice, but a virtue. I hope that everybody practices it. In addition, tolerance will also bring us success. When you meet with difficulties in your work, it is also no use losing temper. You must keep on fighting till the final victory belongs to you.

Be kind. Everyone you meet is fighting a hard battle. The more we know, the better we forgive. Let us be slower to condemn and quicker to forgive. If we knew the other fellow's troubles, we might hesitate to criticize. Go beyond yourself and reach out to other people with a sincere love, respect, caring and understanding of their needs.(515 words)

(Adapted from "Chicken Soup for the Soul")

译文

宽容是一种美德

2004年8月23日，雅典奥运会男子单杠决赛正在激烈进行。28岁的俄罗斯名将涅莫夫第三个出场。他以连续腾空抓杠的高难度动作征服了全场观众，但在落地时，他出现了一个失误——向前移动了一步，裁判因此只给他打了9.725分。

此刻，奥运史上少有的情况出现了：全场观众不停地喊着"涅莫夫"、"涅莫夫"，而且全都站了起来，不停地挥舞着手臂，用持久而响亮的嘘声表达自己对裁判的愤怒。比赛因此中断了，第四个出场的美国选手保罗·哈姆虽已做好上场比赛的准备，却只能尴尬地站在原地。

面对这种局面，已退场的涅莫夫从座位上站起来，向朝他欢呼的观众挥手致意，并深深地鞠躬，感谢他们对自己的喜爱和支持。涅莫夫的大度更加激起了观众的不满，现场的嘘声更响了，甚至一部分观众伸出双拳，拇指朝下，做出不雅的动作。

在如此大的压力之下，一名裁判被迫重新给涅莫夫打了9.762分。可是，这个分数不仅未能安抚观众的不满，反而使嘘声再次响起。

这时，涅莫夫显示出了他非凡的人格魅力和宽广胸襟。他重新回到赛场，举起右臂向观众致意，深鞠一躬，表示感谢；接着，他伸出右手食指做出嘘声的手势，然后将双手下压，请求和劝慰观众保持冷静，给保罗·哈姆一个安静的比赛环境。

涅莫夫的宽容，让中断了数分钟的比赛得以继续进行。

在那次比赛中，涅莫夫虽然没有拿到金牌，但他仍然是观众心目中的"冠军"；他没有击败对手，但他以自己的宽容征服了观众。

当有人和你意见不同或冒犯你的时候，千万不要发脾气。为什么？因为这样做是无用的。你应当宽容并且保持冷静，以免和他争吵。你必须知道宽容不是软弱而是一种美德。我希望人人都能在现实中宽容和忍耐。另外，宽容也会带给我们成功。当你在工作中遭遇到困难的时候，愤怒急躁也是无用的。你必须继续奋斗直到最后胜利属于你为止。

友善待人。你所遇到的每一个人都有自己的难处，让我们在谴责前三思，多一些宽容。如果我们知悉对方的烦恼，我们也许会比较容易地原谅。超越自我，带着真诚的爱、尊重、关怀和对他人需求的理解向他人伸出援手。多一份理解，多一份宽容。

虽然涅莫夫没有赢得比赛，但他的宽容大度却征服了观众。在我们的日常生活中，他人的误解和挑衅就像要向你发起进攻的僵尸一样，这时我们确实应该像魅惑菇一样做到宽容和理解，化敌为友，甚至让僵尸为你而战。其实，对他人宽容不是软弱，而是一种美德，更是对自己的一种保护。

魅惑菇篇
To Leave the Grudge Behind

If I can't leave the grief and grudge behind, in fact I am still in prison

如果自己不能把悲痛与怨恨留在身后，那我其实仍在牢里

Mandela was put into prison for leading to fight against the whites' policy of apartheid (种族隔离). The white ruler imprisoned him in a deserted Ruben Island in the Atlantic Ocean for 27 years. At that time Mandela was already old, but the white ruler still cruelly maltreated him like a young prisoner.

Mandela was detained (扣押) in a "zinc-sheeted room" of the total concentration camp. In the daytime he smashed the large blocks into the stone stocks in the quarry (采石场). Sometimes he went into the icy sea to fish for kelp (海藻) or mined the lime — every morning he lined up with the other prisoners to the quarry, and then was untied the fetters and dug the limestone with a sharp pick and shovel in the large quarry. Because he was an important criminal, Mandela had three guards altogether. They were not friendly, always finding various reasons to maltreat him.

No one imagined after he was out of prison and elected president in 1991, Mandela's action in his inauguration (就职典礼) shocked the whole world.

After the presidential inauguration began, Mandela got up and addressed to welcome the guests. He in turns introduced the political leaders from the countries of the world, then he said he was deeply honored to receive so many distinguished (杰出的) guests, but what he was most pleased was the three guards who guarded him first in Ruben Island prison also turned up. Immediately, he invited them to get up and introduced them to all the guests.

Mandela's open mind and spirit of tolerance made those white people who had cruelly maltreated him for 27 years ashamed while all the people present were filled with deep esteem. Watching the aged Mandela stood up slowly and respectfully saluted the three guards who had guarded him. All the guests present and the whole world calmed down.

Later, Mandela explained to his friends that when he was young, he was quick-tempered and irascible (易发怒的). It was the life in prison that made him learn how to control his emotion, so he could survive. The years in prison gave him time and encouragement and made him learn how to deal with the pains he had encountered. He said that thanksgiving and tolerance often originated from the pain and tribulation (苦难), so we must train through the terribly strong willpower.

On the day he was released, he was calm."When I walk out of the prison to the prison gate leading to freedom, I have made it clear that if I can't leave the grief and grudge behind, in fact I am still in prison."

Forgiveness is a virtue of human beings. It allows us to enjoy the warmth of the sunshine and can bridge the gap of human relationships. Forgiveness, which can be considered as tolerance and as a kind of self-restrained behavior, is needed in every part of our lives. Forgiveness can also be regarded as a civilized behavior.

译

文

It refers to a good way in which we sincerely and genuinely show politeness, kindness, friendship and respect to people.(515 words)

(Adapted from "Chicken Soup for the Soul")

把怨恨留在身后

曼德拉因为领导人民反对白人统治者的种族隔离政策而被捕入狱，白人统治者把他关在一个荒凉的大西洋小岛——罗本岛上长达27年。当时曼德拉年纪已经很大了，但白人统治者依然像对待年轻犯人一样残酷虐待他。

曼德拉被关押在一个封闭集中营的"锌皮房"里。白天他得在采石场里把大石块碎成石料。有时他要下到冰冷的海水里捞海带，有时也要干采石灰的活儿——每天早晨跟其他的犯人排队到采石场，然后被解开脚镣，在一个很大的石灰石场里用尖镐和铁锹挖石灰石。因为曼德拉是要犯，所以有三个看守。他们对他并不友好，总是寻找各种理由虐待他。

谁也没想到，1991年曼德拉出狱当选总统后，在就职典礼上的举动震惊了整个世界。

总统就职仪式开始后，曼德拉起身致辞，欢迎来宾。他依次介绍了来自世界各国的政要，然后说，能接待这么多尊贵的客人，他深感荣幸，但他最高兴的是，当初在罗本岛监狱看守他的3名狱警也能到场。随即，他邀请他们起身，并把他们介绍给所有来宾。

曼德拉的博大胸襟和宽容精神，令那些残酷虐待了他27年的白人感到羞愧，也让所有到场的人肃然起敬。看着年迈的曼德拉慢慢站起，恭敬地向三个关押他的看守致敬，在场的所有来宾以至整个世界都静了下来。

后来，曼德拉向朋友们解释说，自己年轻时脾气不好，很容易发怒生气，正是狱中生活使他学会了控制情绪，因此活了下来。牢狱岁月给了他时间和鼓励，也使他学会了如何面对所遭遇的痛苦。他说，感恩与宽容常常源自痛苦与磨难，必须通过极大的毅力来培养。

获释当天，他很平静："当我走出牢房，迈过通往自由的牢门时，我已经清楚，如果自己不能把悲痛与怨恨留在身后，那我其实仍在牢里。"

原谅是人类的一种美德。它能使我们感受到阳光般的温暖，也能抚平人与人之间的隔阂。原谅被认为是一种宽容，同时它也是一种自律，我们的生活中都需要它。原谅也是一种文明的举止。换句话说，它也是一种真诚地表示我们的礼貌、善良、友谊和尊敬的良好途径。

曼德拉非常大度地谅解了曾经虐待他的狱警，从而赢得了世人的尊重。别人无意或者有意对你的冒犯就像僵尸一样要吞噬你的大脑和心灵，这时你能否和魅惑菇一样谅解他们呢？毕竟僵尸吃植物是他们生存下去的手段啊！学会谅解，谅解是对自己性格和意志的一种磨砺，更是一个人成熟的重要标志之一。如果你学不会谅解，总是揪住别人的错误不放，那你就是把自己关在怨恨的牢笼之中。

之
三

魅惑菇篇
The People in the Town

Do kindness and you have kindness; do bitterness and you have bitterness.

与人为善，收获友善；与人交恶，徒留怨恨。

A young mother was moving to a small town. She wanted to make sure if it would be a good place for her to raise her two small children.

On the outskirts (郊区) of town was a gas station. The young mother pulled over and went in. The gas station was empty. The only person she could see was the woman working behind the counter. She was reading the newspaper. The young woman approached to her.

"Excuse me, I was wondering," the mother asked, "What kind of people live there?" The woman behind the counter gave the mother an appraising (评估的) glance. "That is an interesting question, " she replied, " Why do you want to know?"

"I really want to move here, " the young mother said, "And I come from the city. I want to make sure if I've made the right choice."

The gas station attendant (服务员) nodded, "What were the people in the city like?"

The young mother smiled, "People in the city are warm and welcoming. They are friendly and caring. They all seem to be good people. I just want to find good people like them to settle in with."

"Well," the woman behind the counter said, "I think you will be very happy here, I think you will find the people in this town to be as nice as those city folks."

The young mother was pleased, she bought some cold drinks for her children, thanked the gas station attendant for her time, and left.

Another car pulled up. A man got out and walked inside. He found some cold drinks for his family and came to the counter. The man started to ring up his purchase. "Excuse me, I was wondering," the man continued. "What kinds of people live there?" The woman behind the counter gave the man an appraising glance. "That is an interesting question," she replied, "Why do you want to know?"

"Well, you see," the man said, "I really want to move to a small town like this. I want my family to be happy. I just want to know if I've made the right decision."

The woman nodded. "What are the people like where you're from?" She asked.

"Well," the man replied, shaking his head, " What a lousy (讨厌的) place to live. The people are all stupid and ignorant (无知的). They've the worst drivers on the planet. There isn't a day that goes by that I'm not yelling at someone for driving like an idiot. I can't stand that place. What a bunch of losers!"

"Hmm," said the woman behind the counter, "I think you would be very miserable here. I think you would find the people in this town to be same as those folks."

The man thanked the woman who saved much trouble for him, and went out to his car with the cold drinks. When he pulled back on to the highway, he went back in the direction he'd come from.

Through the story we can understand: do kindness and you have kindness; do bitterness and you have bitterness.(565 words)

(Extracted from "每晚读一篇：哲理英文")

小镇上的人

有一位年轻的母亲准备搬到一个小镇上去住。她想确定一下那个地方是否适合她两个孩子的成长。

小镇的郊区有个加油站。年轻的母亲把车停在路边，走了进去。加油站空荡荡的，她只看到一位女服务员在柜台后面看报纸。年轻的母亲走了过去。

"你好，我想知道，小镇里都住着些什么样的人呢？"这位母亲问道。柜台后的服务员打量了这位母亲，回答说："这个问题很有趣，你为什么想知道呢？"

"我很想搬到这来，"年轻的母亲回答说，"我从城里来，我想知道我的选择是不是正确的。"

加油站的服务员点了点头，问道："那城里的人怎么样？"

年轻的母亲笑着回答说："城里的人都很热情、好客，他们友好而充满爱心，都是好人。我就想找到像他们一样的好人一起居住。"

"噢，是吗？"柜台后的那位女服务员边点头边回答说，"那你住在这儿的话一定会开心的。你会发现这里的人和城里的人一样友善。"

年轻的母亲很高兴，给她的孩子们买了一些冷饮，谢过加油站的服务员后便离开了。

又有一辆车停了下来，一位男士下车走进了店铺。他为家人选了些冷饮来到柜台前，准备结账。"你好，我想问一下，"男士接着说，"都是些怎样的人住在这个小镇上？"

柜台后的女服务员打量一下这位男士。"这个问题很有趣，"她说，"你为什么想知道呢？"

"嗯，是这样的，"男士回答说，"为了让我的家人过得幸福，我很想搬到像这样的小镇上生活。我想知道我这个选择是不是正确。"

女士点点头。"你现居住的地方人怎么样？"她问道。

"唉，"男士摇着头无奈地回答道，"糟糕透了，那里的人都愚蠢无知。他们的驾车技术是这个星球上最烂的，我每天都要为那些白痴一样开车的人而大发雷霆。我再也忍受不了那里了，一群窝囊废！"

"嗯，"柜台后的女服务员说，"我想你住在这里会很悲剧的，你会发现这里的人和你那边的一模一样。"女服务员回答。

那个男人感谢过帮他省了很多麻烦的那位女士，之后抓起冷饮回到车上去了。他上了高速路，调转车头朝着他来的地方驶去。

通过故事我们能够明白这样一个道理：与人为善，收获友善；与人交恶，徒留怨恨。

你怎么对待别人，别人也会怎么对待你。以积极的态度来对待周边的人或事，你也会有一个愉悦的心情；以怨天尤人的态度对待周边的人或事，你也会终日郁郁寡欢。迷惑菇把僵尸看成自己的朋友，而僵尸最终确实也成了它的朋友。

之
四

魅惑菇篇
The Cracked Water Pot

> But if we will allow it, the Lord will use our flaws to grace His Father's table.
>
> 只要我们能接受自己的瑕疵和缺点，总会有人来利用它们来做些有用的事情。

A water bearer in India had two large pots, each hung on each end of a pole which he carried across his neck. One of the pots had a crack in it, and while the other pot was perfect and always delivered (运送) a full portion of water. At the end of the long walk from the stream to the master's house, the cracked pot arrived only half full.

For a full two years this went on daily, with the bearer delivering only one and a half pots full of water to his master's house. Of course, the perfect pot was proud of its accomplishments (成就), perfect to the end for which it was made. But the poor cracked pot was ashamed of its own imperfection, and miserable that it was able to accomplish only half of what it had been made to do. After two years of what it perceived to be a bitter failure, it spoke to the water bearer one day by the stream, "I am ashamed of myself, and I want to apologize to you."

"Why?" asked the bearer. "What are you ashamed of?"

"I have been able, for these past two years, to deliver only half my load because this crack in my side causes water to leak (漏) out all the way back to your master's house. Because of my flaws, you have to do all of this work, and you don't get full value from your efforts," the pot said.

The water bearer felt sorry for the old cracked pot, and in his compassion (同情) he said, "As we return to the master's house, I want you to notice the beautiful flowers along the path."

Indeed, as they went up the hill, the old cracked pot took notice of the sun warming the beautiful wild flowers on the side of the path, and this cheered it some. But at the end of the trail, it still felt bad because it had leaked out half its load, and so again it apologized to the bearer for its failure.

The bearer said to the pot, "Did you notice that there were flowers only on your side of your path, but not on the other pot's side? That's because I have always known about your flaw, and I took advantage of it. I planted flower seeds on your side of the path, and every day while we walk back from the stream, you've watered them. For two years I have been able to pick these beautiful flowers to decorate my master's table. Without you being just the way you are, he would not have this beauty to grace his house."

Factually, each of us has our own unique flaws. We're all cracked pots. But if we will allow it, the Lord will use our flaws to grace His Father's table. (504words)

(Adapted from "www.kekenet.com")

有裂缝的水罐

印度有一个挑水工，他有两个大罐子，分别挂在肩上的扁担两头儿。其中，一个上面有一道裂缝，而另一个罐子则毫无瑕疵，总是装着满满的一罐水。每当挑水工经过长途跋涉从溪边回到主人家时，带有裂纹罐子里的水就只剩一半了。

这样过了整整两年，这个挑水工每天挑到雇主家的水仅有一罐半。当然，那个完好的罐子为自己的成就甚感自豪。而那个可怜的有裂缝的罐子却因自身的瑕疵而羞愧不已，为自己只能装一半水而痛苦不堪。痛苦了两年后，一天，那个有裂缝的罐子在小溪边对挑水工说："我很惭愧，想向你道歉。"

"为什么？"挑水工问，"你羞愧什么呢？"

"为这两年来只能让你挑回一半的水。因为我身上的这个裂缝，每次你回主人家的路上，水都在漏，到家时就只剩下半罐了。正是我的裂缝，你不得不多挑几次水，也使得你的劳动没有得到应有的回报。"罐子说道。

挑水工对这个有裂痕的旧罐子的烦恼感到很抱歉，他同情地说道："当我们返回主人家时，我希望你能留心沿路那些美丽的花朵。"

的确如此，当他们上山时，这个有裂缝的旧罐子注意到了路旁的野花，它们沐浴在阳光中非常漂亮。它感到了一丝快乐，但到主人家时，它又为自己漏了一半水而难过起来，于是，它再次为自己的失败向挑水工道歉。

挑水工对罐子说："你注意到了吗？你这边沿路都有花，而另一边就没有？我早就注意到了你的裂缝，我就是利用这一点，在你这侧的路边种上花籽。每天，我们从小溪回来时，你就给它们浇了水。这两年，我就采这些漂亮的花朵来装点主人家的桌子。倘若你不漏水，他就没有这么美丽的鲜花来装饰屋子了。"

事实上，每个人都有自己缺点，我们都是有裂缝的罐子。只要我们能接受自己的瑕疵和缺点，总会有人来利用它们来做些有用的事情。

两个水罐中的一个虽然有裂缝，但是挑水工并未放弃它，而是发现了它除了盛水外还可以灌溉路边花朵的作用。因此怀着宽容的心看他人的缺点，说不定我们也能从中找到其自身的优势。这就像魅惑菇用宽容理解去看待僵尸一样，它认为僵尸并不是一无是处的，而是在生态圈中同样扮演着重要角色。

之
五

魅惑菇篇
Weakness or Strength

Life is like a box of chocolates, Forrest. You never know what you're gonna get.

生活就像一盒巧克力，你永远不会知道将来你会得到什么。

Sometimes your biggest weakness can become your biggest strength. Take, for example, the story of one 10-year-old boy who decided to study judo despite the fact that he had lost his left arm in a devastating (毁灭性的) car accident.

The boy began lessons with an old Japanese judo master. The boy was doing well, so he couldn't understand why after three months of training the master had taught him only one move.

"Sensei," the boy finally said, "Shouldn't I be learning more moves?"

"This is the only move you know, but this is the only move you'll ever need to know," the sensei said.

Not quite understanding, but believing in his teacher, the boy kept training.

Several months later, the sensei took the boy to his first tournament (锦标赛). Surprising himself, the boy easily won his first two matches. The third match proved to be more difficult, but after some time, his opponent (对手) become impatient and charged; the boy deftly (熟练地) used his one move to win the match. Still amazed at his success, the boy was now in the finals.

This time, his opponent was bigger, stronger, and more experienced, for a while, the boy appeared to be overmatched. Concerned that the boy might get hurt, the referee called a time-out. He was about to stop the match when the sensei intervened.

"No," the sensei insisted, "Let him continue."

Soon after the match resumed, his opponent made a critical mistake: he dropped his guard. Instantly, the boy used his move to pin him. The boy had won the match and the tournament. He was the champion.

On the way home, the boy and the sensei reviewed every move in each and every match. Then the boy summoned (鼓起) the courage to ask what was really on his mind.

"Sensei, how did I win the tournament with only one move?"

"You won for two reasons," the sensei answered. "First, you've almost mastered one of the most difficult throws in all of judo. And second, the only known defense for that move for your opponent is to grab your left arm."

The boy's biggest weakness had become his biggest strength.

Just like the mother in Forrest Gump said, "Life is like a box of chocolates, Forrest. You never know what you're gonna get." Everything is not absolute, and anything can happen in the future. Sometimes, you don't know when your biggest weakness will become your biggest strength, which brings a great surprise or success to you.(442 words)

(Adapted from "英语床头灯：感悟生活")

译
文

缺陷还是优势

有时你最大的缺陷可能会变成你最大的优势。以一个10岁小男孩的故事为例吧。这个男孩虽然在一次可怕的车祸中失去了左臂，但他仍然决定学习柔道。

男孩开始跟随一个年长的日本柔道大师学习。男孩学得很好，只是他不明白，为什么三个月里老师只教他练习一个动作。

"老师，"男孩终于开口问道，"我是不是应该学些其他的招式呢？"

"这是你唯一知道的招式，也是你唯一需要知道的招式。"教练回答道。

男孩不太明白，却信任他的老师，于是继续练习。

几个月后，老师带男孩参加了他的第一次比赛。令男孩惊讶的是，他轻松地赢了前两场比赛。第三场比赛要更难一些，但是过了一会儿，他的对手开始变得急躁和紧张。男孩熟练地运用他所学会的那个动作赢了比赛。男孩仍惊讶于自己的成功，而他已进入决赛了。

这一次，他的对手更大、更强壮、更有经验。有一阵儿，男孩似乎要被打败了。裁判怕男孩受伤，叫了暂停。当裁判想要就此结束比赛时，男孩的老师阻止了他。

"不要，"老师坚持道，"让他继续比赛。"

比赛重新开始，不久，男孩的对手就很快犯了严重的错误：他减弱了防守。男孩立即用学过的招式压住了他。男孩赢得了这场比赛，也就赢了竞标赛，他成为了冠军。

在回家的路上，男孩和教练回顾了每场比赛的每个动作，然后男孩鼓起勇气问出了他一直想问的问题。

"老师，为什么我只用了一个招式就赢了竞标赛？"

"你的获胜有两个原因，"老师答道，"第一，你基本掌握了柔道中最难学的一个动作。第二，要应对这个动作，你的对手唯一可以做的就是去抓你的左臂。"

男孩最大的缺陷反而成了他最大的优势。

正如电影《阿甘正传》里的妈妈所说的那样："生活就像一盒巧克力，你永远不会知道将来你会得到什么。"世事无常，任何事情都不会是绝对的，有时候你最大的缺陷不知道什么时候就会成为你最大的优势，带给你一个很大的惊喜或成功。

故事中的男孩在教练的帮助下把自己的缺陷变成了优势；同样，魅惑菇也不是绝对地把僵尸看成敌人，而是朋友。任何事情都不是绝对的，劣势也许在一定条件下就会转化为优势，敌人也能成为朋友。"生活就像一盒巧克力，你永远不会知道将来你会得到什么。"所以，像魅惑菇一样善于学习吧，从另一个角度看问题。

乐观、无私的路灯花

之一

路灯花篇
The Price of Miracle

> Tess smiled. She knew exactly how much a miracle cost—one dollar and eleven cents plus the faith of a little child.
>
> 苔丝笑了。她知道奇迹的真正价值：一美元十一美分，加上一个小女孩的信念。

Tess was a precocious (早熟的) eight-year-old girl when she heard her Mom and Dad talking about her little brother, Andrew. All she knew was that he was very sick and they were completely out of money.

"Only a very costly surgery could save him now and it was looking like there was no-one to loan us the money." She heard Daddy say to her tearful Mother with whispered desperation, "Only a miracle can save him now."

Tess went to her bedroom and pulled a glass jelly jar from its hiding place in the closet. She poured all the change out on the floor and counted it carefully. Three times, even. The total had to be exactly perfect. No chance here for mistakes. Carefully placing the coins back in the jar and twisting on the cap, she slipped out the back door and made her way six blocks to the pharmacy with the big red Indian chief sign above the door.

"Sir, I want to talk to you about my brother," Tess said to the busy pharmacist (药剂师). "He's really, really sick and I want to buy a miracle."

"I beg your pardon?" said the pharmacist. "His name is Andrew and he has something bad growing inside his head and my Daddy says only a miracle can save him now. So how much does a miracle cost?"

"We don't sell miracles here, little girl. I'm sorry but I can't help you," the pharmacist said, softening a little. "Listen, I have the money to pay for it. If it isn't enough, I will get the rest. Just tell me how much it costs."

At this time, The pharmacist's brother came, he was a well-dressed man. He stooped down and asked the little girl, "What kind of a miracle does your brother need?" "I don't know," Tess replied with her eyes welling up.

"I just know he's really sick and Mommy says he needs an operation. But my Daddy can't pay for it, so I want to use my money."

"How much do you have?" asked the man.

"One dollar and eleven cents," Tess answered barely audibly. "And it's all the money I have, but I can get some more if I need to."

"Well, what a coincidence (巧合)," smiled the man. "A dollar and eleven cents — the exact price of a miracle for your little brother. " He took her money.in one hand and with the other hand he grasped her mitten and said, "Take me to where you live. I want to see your brother and meet your parents. Let's see if I have the kind of miracle you need."

That well-dressed man was Dr. Carlton Armstrong, a surgeon, specializing in neurosurgery (神经外科). The operation was completed without charge and it wasn't long until Andrew was home again and doing well. Mom and Dad were happily talking about the chain of events that had led them to this place.

"That surgery," her Mom whispered, "was a real miracle. I

wonder how much it would have cost?" Tess smiled. She knew exactly how much a miracle cost–one dollar and eleven cents plus the faith of a little child. (600words)

译文

奇迹的价格

听爸爸妈妈谈起弟弟安德鲁的事情时，苔丝已是一个早熟的8岁小女孩。她只知道弟弟病得很厉害，父母却已经无钱给他医治了。

"现在唯一可以救他的办法就是做手术，但手术费用非常昂贵，没有人肯借钱给我们。"她听到爸爸对满含泪水的妈妈低声而绝望地说："现在只有奇迹可以救他了。"

苔丝回到房间，从壁橱一个隐藏的地方拿出一个玻璃罐子，把里面所有的零钱倒在地上并仔细数了3次，直到确定无误。她仔细地把硬币放回瓶子并把盖子拧好，悄悄地从后门溜出去，穿过六条街区，来到门上有红色印地安语大标志的药店。

"先生，我想跟你说下我弟弟的事情。"苔丝对药剂师说，"他真的病得很严重……我想为他买个奇迹。"

"你说什么？"药剂师问到。"他叫安德鲁，他脑子里长了坏东西，爸爸说现在只有奇迹能救他。所以，请问奇迹多少钱？"

"我们这里不卖奇迹，小女孩，很抱歉不能帮助你，"药剂师稍带温和地说。"听着，我有很多钱，如果这里的不够，我就回去取剩下的，请告诉我奇迹多少钱？"

这时候，药剂师的弟弟来了，他是个穿着很得体的男人。他弯下腰问小女孩"你弟弟需要什么样的奇迹呢？""我不知道，"苔丝的眼泪涌了上来。

"我只知道他病得非常厉害，妈妈说他需要做手术，但是爸爸支付不起手术费，所以我想用我自己的钱。"

"你有多少钱？"这个男人问。

"一美元十一美分，"苔丝用很勉强才能听到的声音回答。"这是我所有的钱，但是如果不够的话我再想办法。"

"真是太巧了，"男人笑着说，"一美元十一美分——正好可以为你弟弟买个奇迹。"他一手拿着小女孩的钱一手紧紧握住她一只戴手套的手说，"带我去你住的地方，我想去看看你弟弟和你的父母，看看我是不是有你们需要的奇迹。"

这个穿着得体的男人就是卡尔顿·阿姆斯特朗，著名的神经外科医生。手术没有支付任何费用，安德鲁回家后不久就康复了。爸爸和妈妈高兴地谈论着这件事情。

"这个手术真的是个奇迹，这到底需要多少钱呢？"母亲低声自语。苔丝笑了，因为她知道奇迹的真正价值：一美元十一美分，加上一个小女孩的信念。

如果没有苔丝的乐观执着信念，身患重病的弟弟安德鲁就不可能得到阿姆斯特朗医生的无私帮助而获救。所以我们不仅要像路灯花一样在需要的时候可以无私地帮助他人，同时也要像路灯花一样在黑暗和逆境中发出自己乐观和执着信念的光芒。

路灯花篇

Attitude Is Everything

> Jerry lived in part because of his doctors, but in large part because of his optimistic and indomitable attitude.
>
> 杰瑞活下来了，部分归功于医生们，但更主要的是因为他乐观坚毅的态度。

Jerry was the kind of guy you love to hate. He was the type of person who was always in a good mood, always up, always had something positive to say. When someone would ask him how he was doing, he would reply, "If I were any better, I would be twins!"

One day, I went up to Jerry and ask him, "I don't get it! You can't be a positive, up person all the time. How do you do it?"

Jerry replied, "Each morning I wake up and say to myself, Jerry, you have two choices today. You can choose to be in a good mood or you can choose to be in a bad mood. I choose to be in a good mood. Every time someone comes to me complaining, I can choose to accept their complaining or I can point out the positive side of life. I choose to point out the positive side of life. Life is all about choices."

I thought about what Jerry said. Soon, I left the restaurant business to pursue my own business. We lost touch, but I often thought about him when I made a choice about life instead of reacting to life.

Several years later, I heard that Jerry had done something you are never supposed to do in the restaurant business: he had left the back door open on morning and three armed robbers walked in, and held him up at gunpoint. While trying to open the safe, he got nervous and his hand slipped off the combination. The robbers got nervous and blew a hole through his hand and then three rights through the middle of his abdomen (腹部). He lay there on the floor dying as the paramedics (护理人员) were called. They rushed him to the local trauma (创伤) center and he was in surgery for 18 hours and intensive cares for weeks, and finally emerged from the hospital a month later with fragments of the bullets still in his body.

I saw Jerry about six months later. When I asked him how he was, he replied, " If I were any better, I'd be twins."

"Weren't you ever scared? Did you lose consciousness?" I asked.

Jerry said, "The paramedics were great. They kept telling me I was going to be fine. But when they wheeled me into the emergency room, I got really scared when I saw the expressions on the doctors, and nurses' faces. They all looked like I was a dead man. I knew I needed to take action."

"What did you do?" I asked.

"Well, there was a big, burly nurse shouting at me, 'Jerry, are you allergic (过敏的) to anything?' 'Yes,' I shouted back. 'What?' she asked. The doctors and nurses stopped and waited for my reply. I took a deep breath and yelled, 'Bullets!' They all started laughing, and I told them, 'Look, I am choosing to live. Operate on me as if I am a living man, not a dead man.'"

Jerry lived in part because of his doctors, but in large part because of his optimistic and indomitable (不屈不挠的) attitude. (547 words)

(Extracted from "英语床头灯：感悟生活")

译文

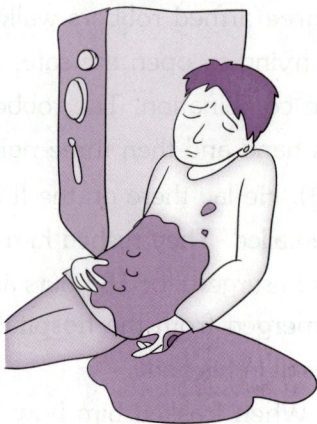

态度决定一切

　　杰瑞真是个讨厌的家伙。他是那种整天心情愉快，乐观向上，经常鼓舞人的人。如果有人问他最近怎么样，他一定会说："我再好不过了。"

　　一天，我去问杰瑞："我不明白，你为什么总能积极乐观，你是如何做到的呢？"

　　杰瑞答道："每天早晨醒来，我都对自己说，杰瑞，今天你有两种选择：心情愉快或郁闷。我选择愉快。每次别人向我抱怨，我可以选择接受牢骚，也可以指出生活的积极面。我选择指出生活的积极面，生活就是这些选择。"

　　我思索着杰瑞的话，不久，我离开餐饮业去寻找属于自己的事业。尽管我们失去了联系，但每当我选择生活而非抱怨生活时，常常会想起他。

　　几年后，听说杰瑞遭遇了一件本不应该发生在餐饮行业的事。一天早上，他没有关后门，三个全副武装的劫匪冲了进去，把枪口对准了他。开保险箱时，他因为紧张，手从锁上滑了下来。劫匪紧张之余，打穿了他的手，又向他的腹部开了三枪。救护车到来时，他躺在地上已经奄奄一息了。人们迅速把他送往当地外伤中心。经过18个小时的手术和几个星期的护理，他终于在一个月后出院了，但体内竟还残留着子弹碎片。

　　大约六个月后，我见到了杰瑞。我问他身体状况时，他说："再好不过了。"

"难道你不害怕吗？当时你失去知觉了吗？"我问。

杰瑞说："医生们很好，他们不断地告诉我，我会好起来的。但当他们把我推到急诊室时，我看到医生的表情和护士的脸时不禁担心起来。因为在他们眼里，我完全是一个死人了。我知道我必须有所行动。"

"你做了什么？"我问。

"一个高大的护士冲我大喊，'杰瑞，你对什么药物过敏吗？''是的。'我回答道。'什么？'她问。医护人员都停下来等我回答，我深深地吸了一口气，喊道：'子弹！'他们都笑了起来。我告诉他们，'看，我要选择活下去，把我当活人而不是死人来做手术吧。'"

杰瑞活下来了，部分归功于医生们，但更主要的是因为他乐观坚毅的态度。

杰瑞遭遇劫匪的枪击，命在旦夕，但是他对生活的乐观和坚毅态度感染和影响了医治他的医生护士，从而使得他也顺利地活了下来。即使环境恶劣，困难重重，路灯花仍然以乐观坚定的态度坚守在黑暗和迷雾中，最终和其他植物们生存下来。路灯花顽强的意志和乐观的生活态度是多么值得我们去学习啊！

路灯花篇

A Lantern in the Dark

> To light up the lamp of our lives can not only brighten others' lives, but also brighten ours.
>
> 点亮属于自己的那一盏生命之灯，既照亮了别人，也照亮了你自己。

On a pitch-dark night, a monk seeking the real Buddha was walking in a desolate (荒凉的) village. In the also pitch-dark road, villagers were coming to and fro silently.

The monk walked round an alley and saw a dim light cast from the depth of the dark alley approaching. One villager nearby said, "Blind Sun(a blind man), is coming."

The monk felt entirely puzzled at the blind man's deed. A blind man was supposed to have no concept of day and night and cannot see everything like birds, flowers, mountains, waters, etc. around him. He could even not know how the "light" looked like. But Blind Sun was surprisingly holding a lantern, which made the monk feel confused and ridiculous (荒唐的). The lantern was approaching with the dim light gradually cast onto the monk's straw sandals (拖鞋). Out of curiosity, the monk asked Blind Sun, "Excuse me, are you really a blind man?" "Yes, I have been blind since I came to this world." The blind man replied.

The monk continued asking, "Since you could not see anything, why are you still holding a lantern?" The blind man said, "It is dark night now, isn't it? I heard that if there is not light on the dark night, all others in the world are also blind just like me. So I lit up a lantern." The monk got the point all of a sudden and said, "So you lit up the lantern to illuminate (照亮) others?" But the blind man replied, "No, I do it for myself." "For yourself?" the monk sank into bewilderment (困惑) again. The blind man, with great calmness, asked the monk, "Have you ever been run into by others on a dark night?" The monk said, "Yes. I was run into by two people just now." The blind man said with a sense of pride, "But I have not all the time. Even though I am blind and cannot see everything, I am holding a lantern in the dark so that I can illuminate others and meantime let others see me. Then they will not run into me due to the dark night."

Hearing the blind man words, the monk felt tremendously enlightened. He could not help looking up to the sky and sighed, "I had been traveling to a lot of places to seek the Buddha and never had I imagined that he is just around me. Our perception of Buddhism is just like a lamp. As long as we light it up, even though we cannot see the Buddha, he can still see us." To light up the lamp of our lives can not only brighten others' lives, but also brighten ours. Only by brightening up others' lives can we truly brighten our own. So please let others light up the lamps of our lives! Only then will we truly seek out the safety and glory we are longing for in the darkness of our lives. (542words)

(Adapted from "www.hxen.com")

黑暗中的一盏灯

一个漆黑的夜晚，一个寻佛的苦行僧走到一个荒僻的村落中。漆黑的街道上，络绎不绝的村民们在默默地你来我往。

苦行僧转过一条巷道，他看见有一束昏黄的灯光正从巷道的深处静静地亮过来。身旁的一位村民说："孙瞎子过来了。"

苦行僧对这个盲人的行为感到迷惑不解。一个双目失明的人，他没有一丝白天和黑夜的概念，看不到鸟语花香，看不到高山流水，他甚至不知道灯光是什么样子的，他挑一盏灯笼岂不令人迷惘和可笑？那灯笼渐渐近了，昏黄的灯光渐渐从深巷移游到僧人的拖鞋上。出于好奇，僧人就问："敢问施主真的是一位盲者吗？"那挑灯笼的盲人告诉他："是的，从一出生，我就是个瞎子。"

僧人问："既然你什么也看不见，那你为何挑一盏灯笼呢？"盲者说："现在是黑夜吧？我听说在黑夜里没有灯光的映照，那么满世界的人都和我一样是盲人，所以我就点燃了一盏灯笼。"僧人顿有所悟："原来您是为别人照明？"但那盲人却说："不，我是为自己！""为你自己？"僧人又愣了。盲者缓缓地问僧人说："你是否因为夜色漆黑而被其他人撞到过？"僧人说："是的，就在刚才，还被两个人不留心撞过。"盲人听了，就得意地说："但我就没有。虽说我是盲人，我什么也看不见，但我挑了这盏灯笼，既为别人照亮，也更让别人看到了我，这样，他们就不会因为看不见而撞我了。"

苦行僧听了，豁然大悟。他仰天长叹说："我天涯海角奔波着寻佛，没有想到佛就在我的身边，人的佛性就像一盏灯，只要我点亮了，即使我看不见佛，但佛却会看到我自己的。"是的，点亮属于自己的那一盏生命之灯，既照亮了别人，也照亮了你自己；只有先照亮别人，才能够照亮我们自己。为别人点燃我们自己生命的灯吧！这样在生命的夜色中，我们才能寻找到自己的平安和灿烂！

盲人夜里点灯是为了别人也是为了自己，路灯花在迷雾中发光，同样也是为了使得植物们能够更好地和僵尸们战斗，因此也就保护了自己。我们在日常生活中是不是也应该像路灯花一样，乐于助人，助人为乐呢？这样做不仅是为了他人，更重要的是为了自己。

路灯花篇
The Warmth from a Cup of Milk

Only if everyone contributes a little to the world, we will have a better future.

只要每个人都献出一点爱心，世界将会有一个更加美好的明天。

One day, a poor boy who was trying to pay his way through school by selling goods door to door found that he only had one dime (十美分硬币) left. He was hungry so he decided to beg for a meal at the next house.

However, he lost his nerve when a lovely young woman opened the door. Instead of a meal he asked for a drink of water. She thought he looked hungry so she brought him a large glass of milk. He drank it slowly, and then asked, "How much do I owe you?"

"You don't owe me anything," she replied. "Mother has taught me never to accept pay for a kindness." He said, "Then I thank you from the bottom of my heart." As Howard Kelly left that house, he not only felt stronger physically, but it also increased his faith in God and the human race. He was about to give up and quit before this point.

Years later the young woman became critically (严重地) ill. The local doctors were baffled (使为难). They finally sent her to the big city, where specialists can be called in to study her serious disease. Dr. Howard Kelly, now famous was called in for the consultation

(专家会诊). When he heard the name of the town she came from, a strange light filled his eyes. Immediately, he rose and went down through the hospital hall into her room.

Dressed in his doctor's gown, he went in to see her. He recognized her at once. He went back to the consultation room and determined to do his best to save her life. From that day on, he gave special attention to her case.

After a long struggle, the battle was won. Dr. Kelly requested the business office to pass the final bill to him for approval. He looked at it and then wrote something on the side. The bill was sent to her room. She was afraid to open it because she was positive that it would take the rest of her life to pay it off. Finally she looked, and the note on the side of the bill caught her attention. She read these words...

"Paid in full with a glass of milk."

(Signed) Dr. Howard Kelly

Tears of joy flooded her eyes as she prayed silently: "Thank you, God. Your love has spread through human hearts and hands."

As a good person, we did something good but asked for nothing return. One day, when you are in trouble, maybe, one good turn deserves another. Only if everyone contributes a little to the world, we will have a better future.(450words)

(Extracted from "www.ebigear.com")

一杯牛奶的温暖

一天，一个贫穷的小男孩为了攒够学费正挨家挨户地推销商品。饥寒交迫的他摸遍全身，却只有十美分。于是他决定向下一户人家讨口饭吃。

然而，当一位美丽的年轻女子打开房门的时候，这个小男孩却有点不知所措了。因此他没有要饭，只乞求给他一口水喝。这位女子看到他饥饿的样子，就倒了一大杯牛奶给他。男孩慢慢地喝完牛奶，问道："我应该付多少钱？"

年轻女子微笑着回答："一分钱也不用付。我妈妈教导我，施以爱心，不图回报。"男孩说："那么，就请接受我由衷的感谢吧！"说完，霍华德·凯利就离开了这户人家。此时的他不仅自己浑身是劲儿，而且更加相信上帝和整个人类。本来，他都打算放弃了。

数年之后，那位女子得了很重的病，当地医生对此束手无策。最后，她被转到大城市医治，由专家会诊治疗。大名鼎鼎的霍华德·凯利医生也参加了医疗方案的制定。当他听到病人来自的那个城镇的名字时，一个奇怪的念头霎时间闪过他的脑际。他马上起身穿过医院的大厅直奔她的病房。

身穿手术服的凯利医生来到病房，一眼就认出了恩人。回到会诊室后，他决心一定要竭尽所能来治好她的病。从那天起，他就特别关照这个对自己有恩的病人。

经过艰苦的努力，手术成功了。凯利医生要求把医药费通知单送到他那里，他看了一下，便在通知单的旁边写了些字。当医药费通知单送到她的病房时，她不敢看。因为她确信，治病的费用将会花费她整个余生来偿还。最后，她还是鼓起勇气，翻开了医药费通知单，旁边的那行小字引起了她的注意，她不禁轻声读了出来：

"医药费已全付：一杯牛奶。"

(签名)霍华德·凯利医生

喜悦的泪水溢出了她的眼睛，她默默地祈祷着："谢谢你，上帝，你的爱已通过人类的心灵和双手传播了。"

作为一个好人，我们也许做过一些不求回报的好事。当有一天我们遇到困难时，我们可能也会得到一些同样的帮助。只要每个人都献出一点爱心，世界将会有一个更加美好的明天。

女孩无私帮助过儿时的凯利医生，因此在自己身患重病，无钱医治的情况下却又得到了凯利的慷慨回报，这使我们不得不想到一句话"好人总有好报"，正如路灯花一样，帮助其他植物照亮黑暗，驱散迷雾，使他们更好地和僵尸战斗，同时自己也可以得到同伴们更好的保护。有些时候，帮助别人就相当于帮助自己呀！

之五

路灯花篇
Selfless Love

Who in the world would love us so deeply and relentlessly without asking for any repay? Only our parents!
还有谁会这样笨拙固执、毫无心机地爱着我们？只有我们的父母！

My friend got married. His mother carried two bags of cotton from the countryside by bus and train to his city. My friend felt bitter as well as funny at his mother's deeds. He pointed to the cashmere (山羊绒) and silk quilts and said, "So long as you have money, you can buy anything in the supermarket. There is no need for you to carry so much cotton here in such a long way."

But his mother insisted and said, "The cotton of this year is light and warmth-keeping. Have a try and you will know!"

Maybe every parent is the same, caring for their children with relentless (持续强烈的) love without caring about whether they know or like it.

This early spring, I went to visit my mother. We had dry beans stew, eggplant salad bar, sauce radish for our dinner, all of which were dried by my mother last autumn and tasted wonderful. I loved the dishes to my heart's content and could not help praising them again and again.

After a few days, my mother, who seldom visited us, came to my home and unpacked her bag, smilingly taking out bags of dried eggplants, dried beans and dried vegetable. She told me that I left so hastily last time that she forgot to give me some of these foods.

I was speechless at that time. Due to my casual compliment (赞美) on her food, my mother , a nearly 60-year-old lady, by taking three buses from the west of the city to the east, came to my home with the food I liked.

My pretty girlfriend had a failed marriage in the past. After divorce, her parents shed the deepest protection and care to her by helping her attend to the child and offering financial aids. Her parents' love made her pull herself together.

Nonetheless, her father, an honest and upright old man, after hearing his ex-son-in-law got promoted in his company, felt terrifically irritated and went to his company to question his boss why a philandering (沾花惹草的) man with corrupt conducts could get promoted.

That night, my girlfriend cried heavily in front of me. I asked her whether it was her father's stupid deeds that made her feel humiliated (感到羞愧的). But she said that she felt guilty for her dad and that though the rest of the whole world betrayed her, her old father would still back her up and help her get the justice she deserved, just as when she was young and the neighboring boy grabbed her ball, her father would get it back for her.

Now we have grown up so much so that we could support our family and have our own children. But in our parents' heart, they are still worried that we do not have sufficient quilts and dried vegetables. They would not feel troubled to bring all these to us regardless of long tough journey. They even would not like us to suffer a bit and try all means to protect us .

Who in the world would love us so deeply and relentlessly without asking for any repay? Only our parents! (529words)

(Extracted from "www.59edu.com")

译文

无私的爱

朋友结婚。母亲从乡下背了两床七斤重的棉絮,坐火车、汽车,辗转而来。朋友哭笑不得,指着满床的羊绒被、蚕丝被说,只要有钱,商场里什么样的被子买不到,非要这样折腾?

母亲固执地辩解:"这是今年的新棉花,轻巧保暖,你试试吧,试试就知道了。"

父母就是这样了。用执拗的心爱着子女,不管他们是否在意,是否领情。

这个早春,我去探望妈妈。晚饭,吃的干豆角炖肉,凉拌茄条,酱萝卜条……都是妈妈头年秋天晒的干菜。嚼来滋味悠长,有阳光的味道。我吃得满心欢喜,随口赞了数声。

隔了几日,平时很少上门的妈妈突然来了,笑眯眯地解开包袱,用塑料袋包得严严实实的是茄子干、干豇豆、花菜干。妈妈说,上回你走得急,我忙得忘了给你装了。

我无语。就因为我心血来潮的一句话,竟然让快六十岁的老人倒了三趟车,从城西到城东,特意跑来。

漂亮的女友有过一段失败的婚姻,离婚后,父母给了她最深的庇护。帮她带孩子,给她经济援助。双亲的关爱让她重新焕发了生活的信心。

可是,她的父亲,那个温和耿直的老人,却在听到昔日女婿升迁的消息后,抑制不住愤怒,跑到那人的公司质问领导,为什么一个拈花惹草、品行败坏的人会得到提拔?

那夜,女友在我面前痛哭流涕。我问,是她父亲愣头愣脑处理问题的方式让她觉得丢脸吗?女友说,她只是心疼年已70的父亲。纵使整个世界辜负了她,年迈的父亲依然会为她讨还公道,就像年幼时,邻家的男孩抢了她的皮球,父亲帮她要回一样。

是啊,就算我们早已成年,强壮到足以支撑起一个家,生儿育女,可在他们心里,依旧会担心我们没有棉被盖,没有干菜吃,路途迢迢,不怕麻烦地给我们送过来;甚至舍不得我们受半点儿委屈。

还有谁会这样笨拙固执、毫无心机地爱着我们?只有我们的父母。

上面的三个小故事是不是让大家想起含辛茹苦抚育自己长大成人的父母,他们的爱就是这么默默无闻、不求回报,他们的爱也是世界上最无私的爱了。父母唯一希望的就是自己的子女晚辈能够健健康康快快乐乐地成长。这岂不是正如路灯花一样?它们在危险的黑夜和迷雾中默默地发光,奉献出自己,让伙伴们能更好地跟僵尸战斗,从而保护自己的家园。